REVISED AND EXPANDED EDITION

NAVIGATING THROUGH THE WILDERNESS

How I made it through the Deserts of the Sahara and the Mediterranean Sea to Europe

DANIEL HABTEY

Navigating Through the Wilderness: How I Made it through the Deserts of the Sahara and the Mediterranean to Europe

ISBN: 978-9785904291

Scripture quotations marked, unless otherwise indicated, are taken from the Holy Bible, either the New International Version or the New King James Version.

Daniel Habtey's book titles may be purchased in bulk for educational, ministerial, business, fundraising, or sales promotional use. For more information, please email d.habtey@gmail.com

Printed in the United Kingdom

Published by

YPN Publishing and Media, LLC
Leading International Publishing and Media Group
30 N Gould Street, Sheridan, WY 82801 USA

3A/2B Kano Crescent Agbara Estate, LA, NG

Mobile: +2348023768604
Email: admin@ypnpublishers-media.com
Web: www.ypnpublishers-media.com
@ypnpublishers
@ypnpublishers
Ypnpublishingmedia

TABLE OF CONTENTS

DEDICATION

I would like to extend my heartfelt gratitude to my beloved wife, Senayit Alem, who has been my unwavering companion throughout the years. This book is dedicated to her as a token of my profound appreciation. For the past 21 years, she has been a constant source of inspiration and blessing in my life.

Senayit, your patience and wisdom have always amazed me. I am deeply grateful for your friendship, your role as a loving wife, and your dedicated motherhood to our three beautiful children, Abseri, Miellaher, and Adoniram. The words of Proverbs 31:26 resonate deeply when I think of you: "She speaks with wisdom, and faithful instruction is on her tongue."

I am blessed to have you as my wife, dear friend, and the loving mother to our children.

ACKNOWLEDGEMENT

I would like to express my gratitude to the pioneers of the Swiss Nile Mission organisation in Switzerland, which is now known as Mission Am Nil International. I wouldn't be the person I am today without them. The experience of writing a book about my life has been surreal, to say the least. I'd like to express my gratitude to everyone on the YPN team who assisted me. I would like to extend a special thank you to Professor Psalm for coming in every day to assist authors in transforming their ideas into stories, as well as my gratitude to the ever-patient publishing team for their editorial assistance, the insights they brought, and all the support they gave me. I am truly grateful. My previous affiliation was with Elim Huddersfield, where I served as a pastor. Because of this, Rev. Michael Reid and the rest of the team have my sincere gratitude for all the hard work and support they provided. I will never forget it. Because of CAM and Elim Missions, the work that needs to be done in missions has been made possible. Please accept my gratitude, and a special mention goes out to Dr David Garrard, Andrew Ramsey, and Rev Ian Hesketh. It is a privilege to have the artwork for the front and back covers designed by YPN Publishing & Media. In closing, I would like to express my gratitude to everyone who has helped me along the way to reach this point, including but not limited to: Dr Andrew and Susan Lockett, Rev. Peter and Kath Hannam, Simon and Sharon Leek, Stuart and Cheryl Sharp, Claire and

Adrian Jones, Temesghen Debesai, Dr Masresha G. Medhin, Rev. Nega W. Semaet, Eskindir Abed, Yoseph Joe Alem, Elsa H. Mariam, John Alula, Dr. Sirak, Martha Nguse, Natalino Giovanni, Aster & Daniel G. Tesfay, Hewan Abraha, Rev. Temesghen Fissehaye and Caz Graham. Thank you for having faith in what I stand for, and I hope that you will acknowledge my appreciation. In conclusion, I would like to express my deepest gratitude to the source of every gift, my God, my Lord Jesus Christ, and my Saviour. I am grateful that you were the driving force behind the transformation of my life from darkness into a wonderful light.

FOREWORD

The story of Daniel is about a long and difficult journey that is full of both highs and lows. However, it is also a testament to both his dogged determination, tenacious spirit, and the steadfastness of God, who has been there for him every step of the way and guided him to where he is today. This story is meant to serve as a challenge to anyone who believes that life is unforgiving and so difficult that they have no choice but to give up. It demonstrates that there is no obstacle that cannot be overcome if one chooses to walk hand in hand with Christ, who will never fail them.

Dr. David Garrard
Director at CAM International

FOREWORD II

Many people go through life resigned to the circumstances that have been imposed on them. They are unaware of the fact that they have untapped potential waiting to be developed, and as a result, they are overly critical of themselves. Because of this, I have a lot of respect for Pastor Daniel Habtey. He refused to take what life had in store for him and accept it. He was aware that he was destined for great things, and as a result, he focused inward in order to bring out the best in himself. In the midst of his struggles, he came to know Christ, and his devotion to Jesus was unwavering. He became aware of his talent for music and began employing it as a means of worshipping the Lord. I believe that he should serve as an example for people of African descent everywhere, particularly Eritreans. This man has an incredible amount of zeal and passion for his belief in God as well as his belief in himself, which is what has brought him to the place he is today. I believe that whoever picks up this book has the ability to triumph over challenges and realise their full potential despite the odds against them. If Pastor Daniel was able to accomplish it in spite of all the difficulties in his life, then so are you.

Dr. Rev. Temesgen Fissehaye is a world-renowned leader and is in high demand as a speaker. He is also recognised as a global educator, evangelist, instructor, prolific coach, trainer, mentor, and author.

FOREWORD III

Habtey is a man who is an example of someone who has genuinely followed God and has been successful as a result of doing so. When you take into account everything that he has been through, you realise that his book is a treasure from which you can glean information that is of great value. You will realise why Habtey was selected as the recipient of the African Humanity Legacy Icon 2022 award once you have finished reading this book. You will be able to see God's hand at work in the life of this man. This book is captivating from the very first page to the very last.

As the global leader of civility across the world, I would recommend this book to any organisation that is interested in motivating people to advance further and live the lives of their dreams.

Dr. Clyde Rivers

HRH Okogyeman Kobina Amissah I
World Civility Leader, President of iChange Nations, and a world-renowned leadership trainer who has been training leaders for over 25 years he created an impressive list of qualifications that he requires from his students and does not hesitate to give feedback on how they are doing in order to help them grow as individuals or improve certain skills, such as listening more effectively.

FOREWORD IV

Over the past decade and a half, Daniel has been a close friend and ministry colleague of mine. His life story has always been an encouragement to me, as it demonstrates the grace of God through incredibly difficult circumstances. A further source of encouragement is not only the fact that more people will hear his story as a result of this book but also the manner in which he provides insight into the important life lessons he has learned as a result of his challenges and how we, too, can learn from them. I pray that as you read this book, God will transform you into the likeness of Jesus Christ, just as He did with Daniel.

Rev. Michael Reid

Senior Pastor Elim Huddersfield

FOREWORD V

Daniel Habtey is an extraordinary individual with an extraordinary life story. This gripping and riveting account traces his journey from failure and hardship all the way to success, and from hopelessness all the way through the ordeal. The life and message of Daniel will motivate many people to have faith in and trust in the God who is still changing people's lives today.

Rev. Chris Cartwright, General Superintendent of Elim Pentecostal Churches.

FOREWORD VI

Daniel Habtey has been a friend, a singer, and a guide for me throughout our time together. His life is a living testimony of the transforming power of God's mercy and the spirit of triumph that he possesses. Reading his book will, without a doubt, instil a sense of optimism and motivation in the reader.

Helen Berhane

Gospel Singer, Nightingale Ministry

I recall vividly the day I decided to cross the border.

I can pinpoint the precise moment.

My internal state was tense.

My thoughts were scattered all over the place.

My heart was racing as I debated whether or not I should do it.

My mind was jumbled with the thought,

"What if I am caught?" I wondered.

"What if I fall into the hands of a brutal government?"

"What if I end up in the custody of a cruel government?"

Would it result in life imprisonment or the death penalty?

Is it all worthwhile in the end?

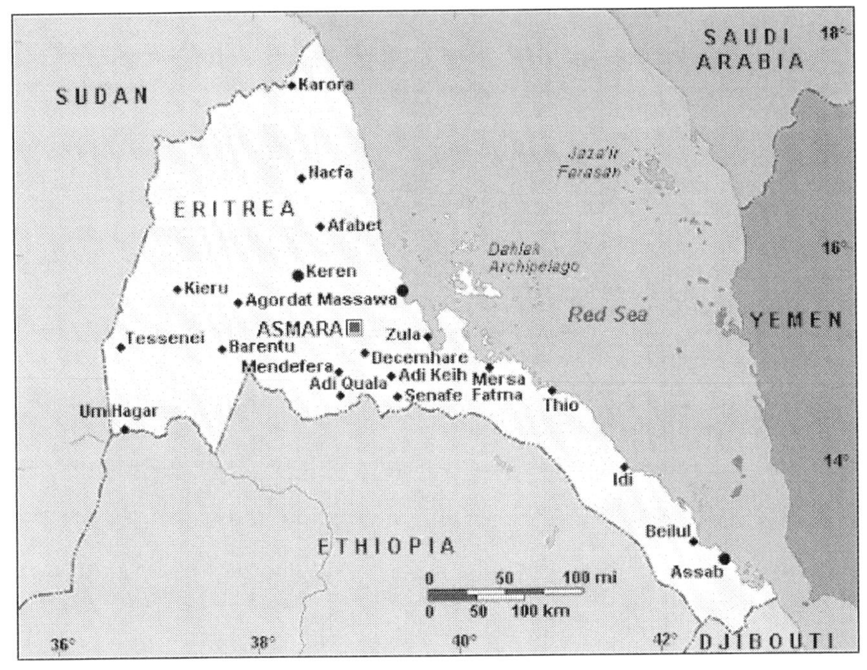

Eritrean cities and towns mentioned in the book.

INTRODUCTION

During the war between Eritrea and Ethiopia from 1998 to 2000, tens of thousands of people on both sides lost their lives in a conflict that was entirely unnecessary. The two nations fought over a small border town called Badme. The Eritrean government subjected me to accelerated training at a military base before sending me to the front lines. Despite spending eight months in hiding to avoid participating in the war, I ultimately had no choice but to report for duty. I despised the training, especially because I believed the war was avoidable, and I had already lost my father to the struggle for Eritrea's independence.

As a result of my father giving his life for the greater good of his country when I was still a young child, I did not have the opportunity to grow up with a biological parent. I deeply longed for his paternal love and guidance as I developed into an adult. Now, I was being asked to make the same sacrifice, rather than take pleasure in the freedom that he had given his life to achieve.

I had a deep love for my nation, but it didn't seem right. Even though relocating outside of Eritrea was never one of my primary goals, I eventually came to the realisation that it was impossible for me to continue living there. Therefore, I made the decision to run away from the military barracks in the hope of finding a better life that included freedom and dignity.

It encouraged me to keep going when I saw that there were three of us trying to get away from there. We started the journey with nothing more than a few biscuits and a small amount of water. Even though we did not know when we would be in a secure location, we maintained an upbeat attitude. We were in a hurry to get away from 'Sawa', the military camp, as soon as humanly possible, so we walked quickly. But it seemed like we weren't making much headway. It was a day with a lot of sunshine and a high temperature, and the ground was sandy since we were in a lowland region.

The three of us were totally alone as far as the naked eye could see, but we were able to make out the distinct sound of gunshots in the distance. I couldn't help but keep looking behind me, certain that some soldiers were following close behind us.

After a while, we made the decision to seek refuge in a rocky cave, and there we remained for nearly the entirety of a single day. We were paralysed by the terror of imminent death, and any glimmer of hope vanished almost immediately. Someone among us commented that because we had committed such an idiotic error, there was no way that we would be able to cross the border without being discovered by the military border patrol. Instantaneously, I was brought back to the heinous "shoot to kill" policy that the authoritarian regime implemented and enforced on anyone who was seen fleeing the country and crossing the border into neighbouring countries.

If they found us, it would be our last day on earth. There was complete silence; nobody had the urge to talk, so we just stood there and looked at each other. After some time had passed, I became aware of the need to make an effort to cheer us up. I couldn't shake the feeling that we were going to make it through this and that the terrible things that had happened to my dad and brother would not befall me.

However, I was hesitant. What if the other people didn't believe what I said? We had to hurry to get back on the road because it was getting dark outside. This time around, the temperature was considerably lower when we set out, and I felt a lot more encouraged and resolved that our journey would be fruitful as a result.

Nevertheless, by the end of the third day, tensions had reached a peak. Because our food and water supplies were running low, we had no choice but to travel during the night to avoid being discovered. When we were walking, we would occasionally hear what sounded like a series of repeated gunshots, and we couldn't help but wonder if this was practice or if it was people being executed for attempting to flee. Following a couple of days of travel, we found ourselves very close to the Sudanese border.

Some of the villagers cautioned us to be careful about who we communicated with because we ran the risk of being taken captive by either the Eritrean government or the Sudanese opposition guerrillas, depending on who we spoke to. It's hard for me to say who would have been the worst option.

After careful consideration, we made the decision to enlist the help of an agent to safely cross the border. The agent agreed to assist us on the condition that we maintained silence, walked swiftly and closely together, and obeyed his orders without delay. Due to my leg injury from my time in the military, I struggled to keep up with the agent's pace. Additionally, the darkness made it challenging, resulting in frequent falls while walking. We continued our journey for a considerable time until finally reaching the borders of Sudan.

Upon our release, we rejoiced in the newfound freedom to talk, laugh, and express ourselves as the agent permitted. Relief washed over me, overpowering the memories of the treacherous path we had just traversed. Little did I know about the trials that awaited me in the Sahara Desert, the Libyan prison, and the Mediterranean Sea.

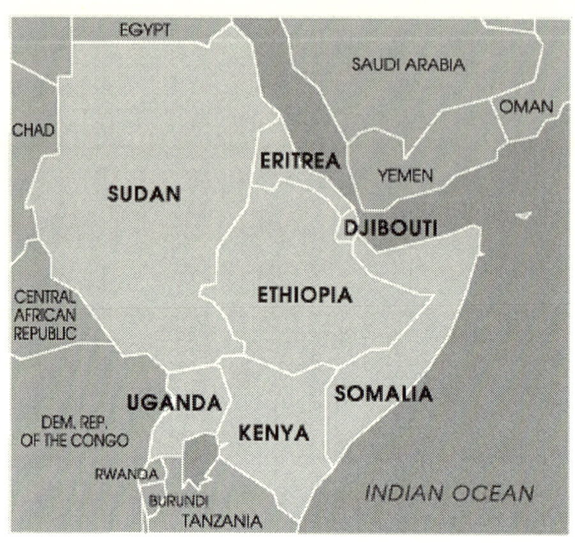

Eritrea and neighbouring countries

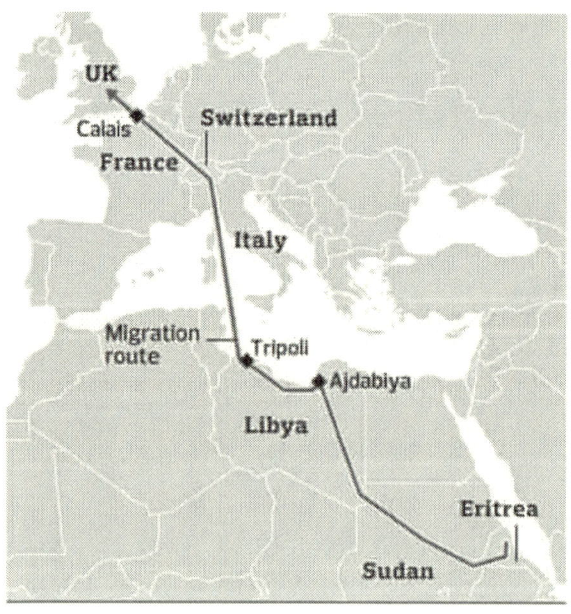

From Eritrea to the UK

Chapter 1

MY CHILDHOOD: A HUMBLE BEGINNING

I had always been perplexed by why people choose to end their own lives when facing difficult circumstances. Do they perceive it as the end of the world? Is it due to a deeply negative and myopic outlook on life that leads them to seek termination? I believe external factors can entirely obscure one's ability to envision their own future. To be honest, I can recall times when I contemplated suicide. It was during a period in my life when I felt as though nothing would improve, and my life seemed stuck in a rut.

The initial chapters of my life were laden with a series of unfortunate events. I was born in Asmara, which is the capital city of Eritrea, a country that is commonly referred to these days as "the North Korea of Africa" due to the infamy of the totalitarian regime that exists there. In the harsh reality of my childhood, tragedy struck with merciless force, claiming the lives of four cherished members of my family in consecutive events. My beautiful mother, my brother, my grand-mother, and my father were all taken from me.

My mother's life was cut short during my infancy due to postnatal complications, leaving me to navigate the world without her gentle guidance from the earliest stages of my life. I was always eager to know what she looked like, and I wondered, but I couldn't find any picture of her. I suppose they couldn’t afford to go to a studio photographer, and the technology of smartphones came too late for her.

My mother departed from this world at a young age; she was around 20 years old. Her name, 'Letezgi,' holds a beautiful meaning, signifying 'a servant of God.' Recently, I had the opportunity to talk to her closest friend and neighbour over the phone from Asmara. During our conversation, she shared incredible insights about my mother that I had never known before. She told me that my mother possessed a gentle grace that seemed to captivate everyone around her. She was full of love and joy for others, with the most radiant smile that could brighten even the darkest of days. She had a way of making everyone feel comfortable and cherished in her presence.

Her friend remarked that she wasn't just beautiful in appearance, but in the very essence of her being—a radiant soul whose inner beauty shone brighter than any outward adornment. Hearing these words filled me with an immense sense of pride, even though I never had the chance to know her myself. Unfortunately, she died when I was about four months old.

My survival was at risk since there was no milk for me to drink; my family members were extremely worried. My father eventually, out of desperation, accompanied me to the village where his mother lived until we finally found her. My grandma started producing breast milk at her old age miraculously to feed me, after she took some traditional herbal medication. Thankfully, I was able to survive.

A little while later, the war between Ethiopia and Eritrea intensified and came dangerously close to the village where we were hiding out. A couple of soldiers were passing by the village. It's possible that my oldest brother, 'Mengistab', mistakenly believed one of them was our father. Curiosity led him to venture outside, under the pretence of needing the bathroom, he managed to slip away. Tragically, this proved to be a fatal mistake. A stray bullet struck him, extinguishing his young life in an instant. My brother was funny, full of energy, and a clever boy. All his hopes and dreams were snuffed out within minutes by a powerful gunshot in a senseless war.

Shortly after, my grandma also lost her battle with grief and poor health and passed away. My grandmother, the one who breastfed me, was truly an incredible woman. Despite being known as the quietest person in our family, she possessed remarkable skills. Her expertise was so renowned that she was often invited to wedding festivities for quality assurance, especially to assess the quantity of food and spices needed.

Reflecting on it now, I realize how fortunate I was to have thrived under her care during my infancy. Her gentle nature and nurturing spirit undoubtedly played a pivotal role in shaping who I am today.

My father placed my older brother, Yosief, and me in an orphanage run by the Swiss Evangelical Nile Mission in Adi-Quala, a town located 86 kilometres to the south of Asmara. He had sent my older sister, Luchia, to stay with relatives in Addis Ababa. He then joined the Eritrean Liberation Front, the army that was fighting to liberate Eritrea from Ethiopia's occupation. Unfortunately, he died in a war to protect his country. I know he visited us only a couple of times before his death. But the one time I remember most was when he visited us in the orphanage, Yosief and I were called, and he was standing by the gate waiting for us to join him. I could see him, a tall figure, and I started to run towards him. But, as I did, I heard an aeroplane fly past and mistook it for a warplane. I made a sharp turn and began to run to hide and take cover. My father laughed and reassured me, "You're safe, my son. This isn't a war plane." We were all safe, and then he hugged me. To this day, his gentle embrace, his humorous laugh, and his kind fatherhood are what I cherish the most.

People speak highly of my father, for his role model and leadership skills. A good-looking man, standing tall, with a masculine physique; he was a well-known hero to many, including our family. However, beyond his physical stature, he was known most for his gentle nature and profound respect for others. Ultimately, he sacrificed his precious life for his country.

After my mother died, my father remarried Alganesh and she had two existing children at the time, Hana and Kifle. I really regret not being able to spend more time with them. My time was limited because I was already at the orphanage at the time, and they lived in the village. I would occasionally pay them a visit on Sunday afternoons; having more siblings was a blessing.

I spent the first few years of my life in the town Adi-Quala, at the Swiss Evangelical Mission Boarding School as an orphan boy. Adi-Quala is a beautiful city with perfect weather. For me, it holds memories of my childhood. It is known for its fertile soil and some historical landmarks. Although some people consider me a villager growing up there, sometimes my wife teases me when I don't know things that she knows. However, the people consider themselves intelligent; in fact, they proudly say, 'A person raised in Adi-Quala is equal to a person who attended university.' It might seem like a big claim but knowing many people from there like my grandfather, they are indeed intelligent. Adi-Quala is a home of many cereals such as Teff grain. Teff is a tiny, special kind of grain that doesn't have any gluten with high fibre and good content of omega and iron. It has great health benefits. People in Ethiopia and Eritrea have been using teff for a long time, making it the main ingredient in their food.

When you grind teff into a powder, you get a flour that's used to make a special type of bread called Injera. This bread is flat and round, kind of like a pancake, and it's a bit sour because it's fermented. However, we love to eat Injera with all sorts of tasty spices—it's a big part of our meals.

Something else special in Adi-Quala known for a traditional homebrew called "Siwa." This popular alcoholic drink is made from home-baked flatbread made of Dagusha (finger millet) and dried African leaves called 'gesso'. The process is quite complicated, but all women know how to prepare it. 'Siwa' has a smoky flavour originating from the toasted flatbread and a bitter and sweet taste after fermentation. People drink Siwa during parties, celebrations, and important events. It's not just a drink—it's a way of showing friendship and kindness to guests.

People in Adi-Quala really enjoy Siwa because it brings everyone together and makes them feel welcome. It's a part of their culture that they cherish and share with others. Most of the time, people go together to "Enda Siwa" for a drink much like going to a pub here in the United Kingdom.

Honestly, I was not a fan of "Siwa." However, my grandfather used to enjoy it a lot. He once told me about an interesting experience he had. A wealthy family invited him to their home and greeted him with a unique type of "Siwa" called "Hitmo." They had let the process ferment for many days, believing that the longer it fermented, the better and stronger its quality became. My grandfather was pleasantly surprised by their generous hospitality and enjoyed the "Hitmo" so much that he drank it until he left their home. It was a memorable experience for him, which he appreciated very much. Apparently, people say it can help with kidney stone problems.

On some Saturdays, we'd break free from the compound and head to the enchanting Adi Keteyo waterfall for a refreshing dip. Venturing out felt like embarking on a mini adventure, cruising past downtown's melodies, and occasionally indulging in sweet treats if our pockets permitted. The waterfall was a lively spectacle; sometimes the breeze teased, causing a playful dance with the water, while other times, it delivered a hearty splash that felt like a close call with baldness. Thankfully, I'm still proudly sporting my locks.

Once upon a time, there was a fantastic swimming spot known as "Sememo," a natural dam that served as the ultimate hangout spot for me and my friends. One day, my two buddies and I decided to enjoy a swim there. However, our day took an unexpected turn when mischievous shepherds decided to play a prank on us by stealing our pants while we were in the water. It was quite a shock to realize we had been stripped of our bottom wear, leaving us in a rather embarrassing situation.

Frantically searching for our missing pants proved futile, and we soon came to terms with the fact that we would have to make the humiliating journey back to our place without them. With only our shirts to maintain some semblance of decency, we embarked on a nerve-wracking sprint through downtown, attracting both laughs and stares from onlookers. It was a challenging experience, especially considering our limited financial resources that prevented us from even affording underwear at the time.

Despite the embarrassment and fear of potential repercussions, we managed to sneak back to our rooms undetected, hoping to avoid any unwanted attention. The close proximity of the orphanage added an extra layer of worry, as we speculated about the consequences of being caught in such a compromising situation. In the end, we were able to retreat to the safety of our rooms, grateful for the modesty our shirts provided as we navigated through a challenging and unforgettable ordeal.

Life in the Boarding School

When I first entered the boarding school, I was just a young child, probably around 3 years old, if my memory serves me right. It was around the year 1976. The directors of the boarding school at that time were a couple from Switzerland, Mr and Mrs Schaffner. My memories of that time are quite faint, but I do recall a few details.

On the day I arrived with my brother, I remember Mr Schaffner tending to the gardens in the backyard of their house. Mrs Schaffner warmly welcomed us and showed us to our dormitory. She was a fast walker, very good at communication and fluent in speaking Tigrinya language, and she was loved by everyone. People remembered by her caring nature and love of Eritrean food 'Shiro', which is made of ground chickpeas.

Even though my recollections are limited, I often hear glowing praise about them from others. They were known to be a remarkable and hardworking couple, dedicated to the welfare and education of the children under their care.

Unfortunately, their time with us was cut short. In 1978, the tranquillity of our boarding school was disrupted by the tumultuous events unfolding in the region. The Ethiopian army, known as the 'Derg,' began their incursion through the 'Mereb' border, which was the closest point to Adi-Quala. It was the same year and place where my father died.

The departure of Mr. and Mrs. Schaffner signified a pivotal moment for our boarding school. Their absence left a noticeable void, ushering in a period of adjustment as we grappled with the changes it brought. However, their unwavering dedication and warmth continued to resonate, shaping the experiences of those of us fortunate to have encountered them during our formative years at the school.

The compound of the Swiss Nile Evangelical boarding school of Adi-Quala is massive compared to other places. A big metal coil fence surrounds it, which can be dangerous if you miss a step and fall onto the sharp edges. I once tried, unsuccessfully, to jump over it and it left me with a scar on my right thigh.

There were two big buildings in the compound: one is the dormitory for the orphans, and the other building is a classroom for the Elementary and Junior school. Each classroom had biblical names on the doorposts, for example there was Kebron, Cana, Gelila, and Bitanya.

My favourite place was the biggest hall called "Bethel", a worship place. The outside of the building was painted with beautiful black and white stones. The inside was filled with long benches, and there was a pedal piano. I remember the serenity of the place and the wonderful songs we used to sing. My first audition ever as a solo singer started there, and my orphan friends remember me by this.

There were two big fields that we used to call the upper field and the lower field. In the summer, we played football, and in the winter, the fields were turned into farms for potatoes, wheat, etc. There were two water wells preserved from the winter rain to provide water for the orphans, for washing dishes and daily use in the absence of the tap water.

Although my time in the orphanage provided me with education, food, shelter, I was a very timid child, prone to quick anger and jealousy of others. The numerous tragedies I experienced at such a young age left me unable to find comfort and recover fully. I grappled with intense pain and struggled to control my emotions. Bottling up negative feelings led to frequent, intense nightmares. In one, a dragon chased me to the edge of a cliff, only for me to wake and realize it was a dream.

Many nights, I'd awaken with tears, sweat, and even urine soaking my bed. Additionally, being born with a cleft lip subjected me to mockery, teasing, and bullying throughout my childhood, fostering feelings of rage, hatred, and shame that lingered into my youth.

One of the orphanage directors, whom we called "the director," constantly reminded me of my helplessness and lack of control over my future, reinforcing my pessimism and exacerbating my feelings.

The director was a commanding figure, possessing a strong presence and a knack for keeping things in order. I'll never forget the distinctive sound of his whistle, always accompanied by the jingle of keys in his hand, which he would playfully twirl. He was undeniably intelligent, having served as a mathematics teacher with a remarkable talent for explaining complex concepts. His neat handwriting was a testament to his attention to detail. However, when it came to management, he struggled, sometimes resorting to harsh disciplinary measures that included physical and psychological reprimands. While he had high expectations for behaviour, he enforced them with unwavering determination, albeit sometimes lacking in leniency.

For instance, I recall one evening vividly, when I was around twelve or thirteen years old. There was a rule at the orphanage requiring everyone to engage in academic pursuits after dinner. Even now, I'm unsure of what I did wrong, but knowing myself, I likely dozed off during study time – I must confess I was never good at studying. Anyways, he entered the room, stood in the middle of it, and yelled my name before telling me to "come out." The tables were arranged in long rows, and I had chosen to take a seat in the middle of the row. When I saw his angry face, I was terrified. As a result, as I stood up, hesitating to come out, I had to squeeze through tight spaces and push my way past other people as he approached me.

When I finally approached him, he grabbed me and flung me into the air upon contact. As I crashed to the ground, he began repeatedly kicking me in the shins. Inflicting a great deal of agony and distress upon my frail body, he then commanded me to return to my desk and continue studying. After venting his anger on me, he stormed out of the room in a rage. It was humiliating for me to walk back to my seat, squeezing past others in silence. Despite the pain and discomfort in every part of my body, the emotional and psychological toll was the most challenging to cope with. This incident occurred in the study room, in the presence of all the students, yet no one dared to stop him. I wonder if someone tried to interrupt him, what would happen? I don't know, but it might be even worse. In a different incident, when I was fourteen years old, there was another time when it was my turn to wash the dishes alongside another orphan named Mehari. The plates were stacked on top of each other, but there was one plate that was malformed and distorted. As a result, it landed on the ground.

The director was outside when he heard the clattering of the dish, prompting him to summon us outdoors to a playground. Upon our arrival, he forcefully threw us to the ground and proceeded to kick each of us multiple times. Finally, he grabbed some clods of soil and hurled them over our bodies. It was a painful and awful experience. After enduring yet another round of painful torment at his ruthless hands, he ordered us to return to the kitchen and finish washing the dishes as if nothing had occurred. We hobbled back to the kitchen to fulfil our responsibilities. When I saw my friend, his face and head were covered in dirt. Trying to conceal my own condition, I attempted to laugh at him, but he quickly pointed out that I too was covered in soil. We both burst into laughter.

Boarding school life was a rollercoaster ride of emotions. There were tearful moments when I questioned everything, and then there were fond episodes fuelled by the hilarious antics of my orphan buddies. I even had those awe-inspiring moments that lit a fire of ambition within me. Looking back, I realize that fending for myself at such a young age played a big part in shaping my independence and resilience. Who knew that navigating through life's obstacles solo could be such an adventure?

When I was growing up in an orphanage, I seem to recall that we were only allowed to consume meat once a week. As a result, it was something that we could consistently anticipate with excitement throughout the rest of the week. But I was a child who had a hard time waiting, and there were moments when a week seemed like an eternity to me. My companions and I were aware that the director typically received a larger portion of the meat than we did. One day, we caught sight of what appeared to be a mouth-watering dish of mutton that had been prepared for him.

There was a momentary lull in the cooking as the chef left the room. After concluding that this was our best chance, we made the decision to sneak in and make a hasty exit without drawing attention to ourselves. At first, I was reluctant, but the encouragement of my close friends and the compelling nature of my hunger ultimately won me over. After that, we were able to sneak into the kitchen, and I quickly grabbed part of the dish prepared for the director and ran away. But the head chef was able to recognise me even though we believed we were being sneaky, because I was a little bit taller and lankier than the others.

We were successful in snatching the dish, but I can't say I enjoyed the meal because of the uneasiness in my stomach, the burns produced by the freshly cooked meat, and the fact that we had to eat while running. This elevated the concept of dining on the go to a whole new level. Because my hands and mouth were badly burned, my overall impression of "Operation Meat Feast" was that the benefits did not justify the risks taken. Somehow, we managed to get away with it. Fortunately, the chief didn't report it to the director. Otherwise, it would have been a different story.

After that, we learned that the other orphan girls had composed a song about us and dedicated it to us. My participation in the activity was humiliating, and the chanting of the song by other people made the situation even more awkward for me. When I think about it now, with the benefit of hindsight, I find it humorous, and I can chuckle about it.

While I was growing up, I didn't have the courage to share my struggles or seek assistance. I had a lot of baggage to unload, but I simply lacked the confidence or the opportunity to do so.

My maternal grandmother, Zehaytu, would often travel a long distance to visit us when we were growing up. She was a very kind, lovely, and gentle woman. I believe she did her best, but the distance made it challenging for her to provide much assistance.

The only person I could relate to and confide in closely was my grandfather, Sengal. He was the most charitable person I've ever met, and his remarks were always reassuring and supportive. Additionally, he had a great sense of humour, was a wonderful poet, and possessed a wealth of historical knowledge. He used to share with me tales of his experiences as an Italian soldier in Sudan and Libya.

During my Sunday visits to my grandfather, he would always make me a cup of tea. To my surprise, he would add chili powder, which intrigued me greatly. Curiosity got the better of me, and one day I asked him why he added chili spice to his tea. He said, "Sweetness is not for a man; a man should enjoy spiciness and sourness. Even life should be a little bit hard for a real man." His response was simple yet profound. He found the tea too sweet on its own and enjoyed the added flavour. This small act revealed the uniqueness of my grandfather and his ability to find joy in the unexpected.

My grandfather taught me many precious lessons. He imparted upon me the importance of offering kind greetings to everyone, regardless of age or gender. He emphasised the significance of showing respect and reverence for all living beings. As a poet and a performer, he ignited my own passion for lyrical expression. I often wondered if my lyrical tendencies were inherited from him. When I was a child, my grandfather wrote a poem dedicated to me. Its verses were filled with love and tenderness, capturing the depth of our connection. Though the exact words have faded from my memory, the sentiment remains etched within my heart. It is a testament to the bond we shared and the profound impact he had on shaping my understanding of life and the arts.

"My grandson Danny, I'm here for you; please do not worry.
You are bright like a morning star.
Fast like a strong tiger,
Surely, I will see you married by January.
And I will celebrate with you joyfully."

He was always able to cheer me up, and he was especially good at it when he noticed that I was being cranky or upset. My grandfather was a very compassionate and thoughtful individual. He had a soft spot in his heart for all living things. Recently, my brother Yosief shared a story with me about how one of Grandpa's hens became unwell and passed away while he was attending a funeral in a nearby town. When he got back and found the chicken, he was so distraught that he mourned the bird's passing for several days. In addition to giving her a dignified burial and funeral, he also composed a poem in her honour. In the poem, he expressed his regret for not being able to shield the chicken from harm and emphasised how much he valued her company.

Meeting Masresha

At the tender age of around eight, life unfolded predictably within the confines of the orphanage. However, a remarkable event occurred that would forever alter my perspective. I found myself unexpectedly thrust into a new realm of experience when a high school teacher selected me to assist in delivering milk and cheese to his hotel room.

One day, amidst the routine of orphan life, a distinguished figure arrived from Addis Ababa to teach at Adi-Quala High School. Masresha, also known for his good character, had a charming personality, and a smile that endeared him to everyone.

The boarding school director, recognizing Masresha's admirable qualities, decided to offer him some milk and cheese as a gesture of appreciation. He assembled a group of five or six youngsters, all around my age, and presented Masresha with the opportunity to choose one among us.

I remember us sitting down, eagerly awaiting Masresha's announcement. At that moment, I found myself praying and competing with the others for this opportunity. Masresha's decision carried weighty significance. He had to select one of us to fulfil the weekly task of delivering milk and cheese to his hotel room. Finally, he pointed his finger towards me and said "you," indicating his choice. I jumped with joy and eagerly accompanied him to see his hotel room, ready to undertake the weekly task.

This chance meant the world to me as it allowed me to step out of the orphanage and into the heart of the city. I couldn't contain my excitement because it was an opportunity to experience life beyond the compound. We were only permitted to leave the orphanage on Sunday afternoons, for a short period of time. Therefore, the privilege of going out for extended periods of time felt like a once-in-a lifetime chance. I certainly looked forward to those days because, at least for those rare moments, I felt liberated from the confines of the orphanage. However, I found this connection interesting and meaningful. His company brought me a great deal of joy and tranquillity since he was such a kind person. Although I have lost track of most of our conversation, I will never forget how much fun I had whenever I was in his company.

He would always ask the hotel desk to bring me a Coca-Cola drink to his room. It was one of the pleasures of getting that rare wildcard to be the lucky one to deliver his cheese. Believe me when I say that, despite how trivial and unimportant it may sound, it was rather crucial.

This was the stuff of dreams for a lonely youngster like me who was living in an institution, a place where love and compassion were nothing more than abstract concepts that existed only in my brain. It wasn't so much about the drink itself as it was about what it stood for: care, compassion, and being treated like a human being who is deserving of life.

Even in the darkest moments, there are often silver linings waiting to be discovered. My heart was filled with such profound gratitude for the fact that there were still decent people in the world on those few occasions when they occurred, and as a result, I began to adjust my mentality away from whining about the challenges I faced throughout the rest of the week. Masresha played a big role in my childhood. His meaningful conversations and surroundings encouraged me to dream and aspire to be a better person. Those precious afternoons were a rarity. I had to endure suffering in the orphanage to look forward to my upcoming appointment with this wonderful man, who was God's messenger. I realized that even the most unremarkable aspects of life deserve gratitude and have the power to improve one's spirit.

After two years, Masresha's contract was terminated, and he had to move back to Addis Ababa, Ethiopia. For me, it was a sad moment. He called me to see him on his last day, early in the morning, to give him farewell before his departure. I remember he encouraged me and prayed over me. Even though I don't recall his exact words, I will never forget his love, care, and intentions for me.

When I was approximately ten years old, my brother was kicked out of the orphanage. The director of the orphanage was not a kind person. He assaulted my brother brutally, making him fall, and as a result his arm was broken. When I saw my brother's agony and life struggle, I was bitter and developed a strong dislike for the director. I rarely found myself not being angry. Everything that went wrong for me was more than enough reason to harbour resentment and refuse to see anything but my own misfortune. When I finally got fed up with everything, two of my friends and I made the decision to run away from the orphanage and join the Eritrean People's Liberation Front, also known as the EPLF.

At the tender age of thirteen, we made the impulsive decision to join an army fighting for independence. Looking back now, it's clear that our choice was immature and irrational, driven by desperation. With the benefit of hindsight and added life experience, we recognize it as an ill-thought-out move on our part. At the time, however, we were blinded by our circumstances. We saw joining the army as our only means of escape from the confines of the institution. In our minds, being orphaned and still alive felt like a curse, and we believed that nobody would notice or care about our absence. Yet we couldn't have been more mistaken about that assumption

It had been just a couple of hours since we went missing when the director of the orphanage sent a search team to look for us outside in the surrounding area. They began their search by dispersing from the orphanage and going in a variety of directions to find the missing children. We had only been able to travel five kilometres before being found out, at which point we were forced to make our way back to the location that we had been working so hard to flee.

My mind was paralyzed by the terror of what we would find upon our return. And if the severe penalty handed down by the director was any indication, then that concern was completely justified. After enduring brutal punishment with ropes and repeated kicking, the director ordered us to engage in disciplinary physical labour for a couple of days. We were tasked with throwing stones from the field, keeping us occupied and preventing the three of us from being together.

When I reflect on my childhood most of the things that happened are enough to make me say life is not fair. Losing family members at a tender age, encountering emotional and physical abuse, bullying and humiliation repeatedly was not a normal incident. I was probably a clueless and reckless child, but I was also aware that I had no alternative outside the orphanage. So, I was trying to behave well to continue living in the orphanage. However, despite my best efforts, as a child when mistakes happen, I was dismissed several times from the boarding school. So, my poor elderly grandfather had to come and beg the director to allow me to return to the orphanage.

I vividly recall the moment when my grandfather approached the director of the boarding school, pleading, "Please help him; this child is poor and has no future outside of this boarding school." I watched as my grandfather knelt at the director's feet, his words piercing me to the core. "Where else is he able to go?" The director didn't seem impressed, but he finally agreed, warning me that it was my last chance. Witnessing my grandfather in such a humbled position filled me with profound embarrassment; I felt responsible for causing this distress.

Though I couldn't change the situation, it made me acutely aware of the need to be cautious and vigilant. I understood the instability of my circumstances and resolved not to put my grandfather in that position again. The ordeal heightened my alertness, prompting me to seize any opportunity that presented itself. Above all, I was determined not to be expelled from the boarding school, willing to explore any avenue beyond its confines. In my heart, I vowed to seize any opportunity without hesitation.

Every Sunday afternoon, I would meet my brother Yosief and his friend Goitom. Both very popular and strong, they possessed kindness and generosity in abundance. My brother and Goitom engaged in physical activities, practicing gymnastics at home, and the results were evident in their physical fitness and overall well-being. Their dedication inspired me, prompting me to follow suit and introduce sports into my routine at the boarding school. While I excelled in sports and acrobatics, my interest deepened thanks to the influence of my brother and his friends.

By the time I reached around fourteen years old, I had embraced a more active lifestyle and began training in karate and boxing. I even crafted two sets of gloves: one for myself and another for my sparring partner. We often had sparring sessions in the orphanage, and my agility allowed me to prevail in most fights.

On one occasion, there was a guy who was driving me crazy. I vividly remember it because he was a few years older than me and relentlessly provoked me. Despite my warnings for him to stop, he continued to antagonize me, and his tactics succeeded in infuriating me. Frustrated and agitated, I eventually reacted violently, catching him off guard and causing him to crash to the ground hard, sliding under the dining room table. In a state of panic, I feared that I had seriously injured him, perhaps even killed him. Overwhelmed with terror, I hastily devised a plan to flee the boarding school and start a new life on the run. However, upon returning to check on him, I was relieved to find that he was conscious and relatively unharmed, aside from some bleeding and swelling.

The thought of facing repercussions for my actions terrified me, as I knew that being reported to the director could lead to my dismissal from the school. Fortunately, the monitor of the boarding school had witnessed the altercation and intervened. He understood the situation, recognizing how the other guy had been tormenting me, and he handled it discreetly without filing a report. This unexpected assistance brought me immense relief, sparing me from the consequences of my actions.

My Turning Point

In the summertime, my friend Meseret would embark on a journey to the enchanting city of Asmara to visit his family. Upon his return, he would regale us with vivid tales of Asmara's charm, painting pictures of its vibrant streets lined with elegant cafes and the mesmerizing play of light on the water fountains. Meseret's stories were rich with the delightful scents and tastes of the city's famous ice cream and decadent cakes, so tantalizingly described that we could almost taste the creamy sweetness ourselves. His accounts left us yearning, especially since Adi-Quala, our hometown, lacked such delectable treats and scenic splendour. Meseret's narratives were more than just stories; they were a feast for our imaginations, igniting a longing for the flavours and beauty that Asmara promised.

More importantly, Meseret shared the most meaningful experiences of spiritual activities and gatherings with youth groups. He spoke passionately about a spiritual revival at Saint Mary Church, organized by an Orthodox youth group. His descriptions piqued my interest and stirred something within me, eventually moving me deeply with his spirituality. I was desperate to escape my miserable situation, seeking answers to my deepest desires and the nightmares that plagued me. Meseret's spiritual experiences offered a glimmer of hope, a beacon of light that promised solace and direction during my turmoil.

After some time, I mustered the courage to ask him, "Why is my life not aligned with the Bible? I don't think I'm enjoying life; my heart is full of anger and misery. Why don't we start a youth group here?" To my surprise, Meseret responded positively. With the help of other friends like Kesete, Habtom, and Kahsay, along with some lovely girls, we managed to assemble a small choir group. We practiced diligently on Saturdays and performed during the church gatherings on Sunday mornings.

One night, as I knelt by my bedside in prayer, I found myself seeking solace from the frightening dreams that had been haunting me. Despite growing older, I had become increasingly troubled by these nightmares, often waking in a state of fear and shame. That evening, I fervently implored the Lord for deliverance from these tormenting visions.

Suddenly, an image of an outstretched arm appeared before me, accompanied by a voice reassuring me: "Come closer to me, and I will assist you." In that moment, a gentle presence enveloped my heart, flooding me with an overwhelming sense of peace, confidence, and relief. It was as if a heavy burden had been lifted from my shoulders, dispelling my anxieties and shame. From that night on, my sleep was so peaceful; no strange or scary dreams occurred. This pivotal event marked a transformative shift in my life.

Eagerly, I shared my encounter with my friends, hoping for validation or similar experiences. However, my friend Habtom wisely reminded me that this was a deeply personal journey. From that moment onwards, I was filled with a profound and unparalleled sense of peace and joy I had never felt before.

Recalling a verse from the Bible, specifically John 14:27 which reads, "Peace I leave with you; my peace I give to you. Not as the world gives do I give to you. Let not your hearts be troubled, neither let them be afraid," I understood the true power of faith and experienced first-hand the mercy and grace of God. This encounter forever changed the trajectory of my life, instilling in me a newfound sense of purpose and gratitude.

This transformation has inspired me to read the word of God diligently and sing passionately. The changes in my life became evident at the boarding school. It feels as though my world has been transformed into something completely new. The joy and comfort I found in Jesus helped me leave behind my past life - the negative feelings, fear, anger, and trauma seem to have been overcome. I have found new hope, purpose, and a sense of mission. It's as if the old me has passed away and a new me has emerged, just like the verse from 2 Corinthians 5:17 says, "Therefore, if anyone is in Christ, he is a new creation. The old has passed away; behold, the new has come."

Even as I embraced spirituality, my past anger issues still lingered at fifteen. One day, a boy at the boarding school around my age challenged my composure post-conversion by provoking me. Remembering the biblical "turn the other cheek" lesson, I offered mine. Shockingly, he smacked me in defiance, shattering my newfound peace. Confused and furious, I grappled with shame and lost control, retaliating, and pinning him down.

It was a humbling moment that showed me I still had much to learn on my journey towards inner peace. My spirituality was tested and found wanting, but it was a valuable wake-up call that reminded me of the work still left to be done.

My friends were incredibly supportive during this time. We spent hours reading, singing, and studying together. One of my favourite verses, James 4:8, stood out to me: "Draw near to God, and He will draw near to you." Inspired, I made a conscious decision to deepen my relationship with God.

As we sang solos together at boarding school, I found their encouragement uplifting. The experiences we shared helped shape my values, transforming me into a calmer, less irritable person who was genuinely kind to others. I embraced the role of peacemaker, often involving myself in reconciliation efforts.

My dear friend Meseret and I took it upon us to resolve disputes between individuals and groups. Recognizing the futility of arguments that stemmed from trivial differences, we worked to foster understanding and unity. Our shared background of growing up in the same orphanage and attending the same compound highlighted the insignificance of such divisions. Serving as mediators within the orphanage brought us a sense of fulfilment as we helped mend relationships and promote harmony among our peers.

As a result of my new adventure, my life has changed significantly. I experienced tranquillity and began to trust God for my life. My inner peace flourished, and I gained a sense of direction and clarity for the future. I also experienced personal growth and strengthened connections with people around me. As I entertained positive visions, dreams, and inspirations, I felt compelled to become a better person. This new way of thinking, which I had begun to cultivate within myself, was gradually taking shape, and I realized that I held the power to shape my own future.

One evening during our ritual gathering, someone shared a verse from the Bible: "For I know the plans I have for you," says the LORD. "They are plans for good and not for disaster, to give you a future and a hope." My heart was greatly encouraged by these words.

On a different occasion, a Catholic priest visited our boarding school from Asmara and sang a beautiful song for us. It was truly uplifting. I recall the priest wearing a brown robe, with light skin and a beautiful voice. It may have been the day that my heart was deeply moved by music, particularly the sound of the guitar.

Leaving the Boarding School

Even though my childhood was undeniably challenging, growing up in the orphanage in hindsight was exciting, filled with joys and brotherhood. The social life we shared was vibrant and heart-warming, with simple pleasures that remain vivid in my memory. Each morning, we would gather for breakfast, savouring the taste of cheese paired with powdered milk or sometimes a comforting cup of tea. Looking back, I believe these humble, yet nourishing meals and physical exercises played a significant role in keeping me strong and fit. It was vital in providing the sustenance needed for our youthful adventures.

Football was our passion, a unifying force that brought us together in spirited competition. We would eagerly take to the field, our young hearts set on victory. The stakes were clear: the winners would earn the coveted reward of our morning cheese, while the defeated would have to endure a day without this cherished treat. Our football team was a force to be reckoned with, and among us, I think Samuel Debesai stood out as a star player. His skill and determination led us to triumph in countless matches, earning him popularity among our group. In the context of today's football world, I often imagine Samuel as our very own Lionel Messi, guiding our team to glory with his football talent.

Samuel and his siblings were exceptionally kind and cooperative to the orphans. I remember once I was so ill, and I don't know what was wrong with me, all I remember is I had been in the bed for a long period of time. By the time I got up from bed I left with skin and bone only. I had only short trousers and it was very noticeable. Mr. Debesai Kassa (Samuel's father) saw my frail shape and was compassionate towards me. He assigned me to dine with his children to help me recover properly as their food was more nutritious. It was such an act of his kindness and credit to his considerate approach.

So, for a couple of weeks, I ate with Samuel's and siblings, which I enjoyed the warmth of the entire family, especially Samuel was a good friend. The meals cooked by his precious mother were incredibly delicious. A friend named Kahsay gave me a pair of long trousers to cover my skinny legs. It really improved my appearance. Looking back now, it was such a beautiful display of heart and love in action.

Beyond the thrill of the game, the bonds we forged in the orphanage have proven to be lasting and profound. The friends I made during those formative years are more than just companions; they are like siblings to me. We have shared in each other's joys and sorrows, forming a tight-knit community built on love and mutual support. When adversity struck any member of our group, we rallied together, offering whatever help and comfort we could provide. This sense of unity and shared responsibility has instilled in us a deep understanding of the importance of community, shaping the way we care for and uplift one another to this day.

In the orphanage, amidst the challenges and hardships, we discovered the true essence of family — not bound by blood, but by the bonds of shared experiences and unwavering solidarity. We laughed together, we cried together, and through it all, we grew together. These memories, etched in my heart, serve as a reminder of the resilience and strength that can emerge from even the most difficult of circumstances. The orphanage was more than just a place of shelter; it was a home where we learned the power of friendship, the joy of simple pleasures, and the enduring spirit of community.

In 1988, I was ready to leave the boarding school and embark on my future career. Aware of potential dangers lurking around me, I was cautious not to jeopardize my life. Though uncertain about my next steps, I felt a strong urge to challenge myself and navigate my childhood wilderness by embracing any adventure that came my way.

One day, a fellow orphan by the name Gezachew, who had studied at a health assistant school in Asmara came to the boarding school with news of an opportunity to study. I welcomed the news along with my other seven orphan friends. While I was excited, I was equally nervous, lacking a strong plan for finances and accommodation. Nevertheless, I believed it was worth trying anything, so I decided to go to Asmara with some money for transportation. This journey was solely for the entrance exam to determine if I was qualified. If successful, it would lead to a two-year training program.

Thanks to my friends' support, I successfully passed the exam. Now, the good news is that I passed, but the bad news is how I'll sustain myself for two years in terms of accommodation and financial assistance. It was quite an adventure, but a decision needed to be made. I could see the challenges mounting, especially in Asmara, being the capital city where things are more expensive compared to Adi-Quala town.

In the end, I made the decision to go to Asmara to pursue my new career and leave the boarding school. Despite being fifteen years old, I felt strong. While nervous to leave my comfort zone, I was also confident in facing the challenges ahead.

However, I left with the most precious thing: the fear of the Lord. Even though I was not sure I was full of confidence and faith in God. So, the boarding school helped me in every part of my life. I believe without the Swiss Evangelical Mission I wouldn't be the person who I am now. God's love and mercy transformed my life forever. My fear was replaced by faith, my shame and sin were redeemed, and the wounds and trauma were completely healed. So, I went to Asmara with strength and boldness.

I would like to mention some people who really contributed to my spiritual journey. Mihreteab B. Yikun and Adanesh G. Meskel used to encourage us continually to be strong in faith. I will never forget their great effort. They were very passionate in modelling Christ-like life. Their effort is not in vain. There was another teacher called Yohannes Okbazion, and his beautiful wife Dehab, they used to encourage us to seek God diligently, and his righteousness. They set up an early prayer meeting to start our day with the Lord.

One of my fond memories is when I used to drink hot tea made by a teacher, Mebrat, who was the mother of my best friend, Meseret. It was a really refreshing time. I used to crave tea because most of the time we only had powdered milk to drink every morning in the boarding school. Her generous approach made me feel special.

Finally, I used to study with a group of people whom I called my friends, and they greatly helped me achieve excellent results. Kesete, Habtom, Maryam, Eden, and Kahsay were true friends and instrumental in my academic progress.

One of the most significant mistakes I made in my young life was having very high expectations of other people, especially the director of the orphanage. With no one else to provide for me, I expected him to fulfil some basic needs and offer guidance for my future. However, I soon realized he wasn't interested in taking on that responsibility. I often made silent demands on my family and others in more advantaged positions, hoping they'd empathize with my difficult childhood and help.

However, I came to understand that this mindset was unproductive and showed a lack of responsibility on my part. No one else was obligated to help me and relying too much on others without taking responsibility for my own actions wouldn't improve my life. Recognizing this, I knew I had to change my approach if I wanted to see progress.

I needed to take charge of my life, accept reality, and cultivate a positive mindset to overcome challenges.

My biggest regret was blaming others for not helping me, rather than accepting the reality of my circumstances. No one else can change the life we're born into, whether it's as an orphan or a prince. It's easy to get caught up in blaming others when we feel like we lack control over our lives, but this only leads to a lack of accountability and personal growth.

I've learned that maturity involves taking responsibility for oneself and helping others, when possible, rather than expecting others to fulfil our needs. Continuously blaming others keeps us stagnant, while taking ownership of our actions allows us to move forward and make positive contributions to our lives and the lives of others.

QUESTIONS AND SELF-REFLECTION FOR PRACTICAL STEPS

Everyone has a story, and I told mine so that we could all learn from each other. My story includes both positive and negative experiences. The bad news is that I can't change what happened in the past, but the good news is that there's a lot to learn from each story, and most importantly, it allows us to apply the principles to improve our lives. The following questions are intended to stimulate your thinking about the chapter's content and assist you in learning some lessons. Please take some time to reflect and absorb useful information. Consider the story's relevance to your own life experiences, let your mind wander, be encouraged to challenge yourself, and look for ways to make the world a better place.

Question 1

What lessons have you learned from this chapter?

Question 2

What kind of losses have you experienced?

Question 3

What principles or lessons will you apply to help you overcome challenges?

Question 4

Do you have anyone who you feel may be able to help you currently? Mention them.

Question 5

Are there ways you can be of help to others too?

Question 6

If you were to change the narrative of your own story, what things would you change?

Chapter 2

TAKING OWNERSHIP OF MY FUTURE

By the age of fifteen, I made the bold decision to embark on an independent journey, assuming full responsibility for shaping a better life for myself. Armed with just enough money from a distant relative to purchase a one-way bus ticket, I bid farewell to my friends, including the director, though his reaction seemed less than impressed. Nonetheless, I ensured to pack a suit to present myself nicely for the journey ahead. I went to the bus station and boarded the bus bound for Asmara to commence my new career as a health assistant. As the driver ignited the engine, I was overwhelmed with mixed feelings. On one hand, I was embarking on an exciting new journey; on the other, I was haunted by the "what ifs" that shadowed my thoughts.

As the journey continued, I couldn't help but contemplate the uncertain future that lay ahead of me. I was consumed with questions and doubts. What if something went wrong? Would this journey be successful? I weighed my options, but one thing remained certain—I was tired of being cast out of the orphanage. Recollections of the director's warnings echoed in my mind, instilling a sense of fear. I had heard stories of former orphans who struggled after leaving the boarding school, and I couldn't shake the feeling of uncertainty about my own future. Despite the trepidation, I knew I had to forge ahead and create my own path.

I remembered my beloved brother Yosief, who had once been an excellent student but seemed to have slowed down after being expelled. Lost in my thoughts, I was suddenly interrupted by a small, beautiful girl waving at me with a smile. I recognized her from a family wedding a few weeks prior, where we had exchanged smiles and playful gestures. Her mother, seated beside her, asked how I knew her daughter, sparking a conversation that eventually led to me becoming a part of their family.

During my uncertainty, her invitation to stay with them as their guest felt like a ray of hope. It was a reminder that amidst the doubts and fears, there were still moments of kindness and warmth to be found, offering a glimmer of hope for the journey ahead. This was one of the incredible miracles God had bestowed upon me.

The beautiful little girl seemed like an angel to me, and her mother's gesture of extending her arm to welcome me was simply indescribable. That evening, the whole family gathered at Mr. Berhane's house for dinner, and everyone greeted me warmly with smiling faces. I stayed with them until I found a place to settle. Their treatment of me was exceptionally kind and beautiful.

When I finally arrived, the splendour of Asmara completely captivated and overwhelmed me. Having spent my formative years at an orphanage in Adi-Quala, I had grown accustomed to a certain environment, and the bustling vibrancy of Asmara was a stark contrast. The city was bigger, noisier, and busier than anything I had ever known.

Embarking on a journey from a humble town to the magnificent capital city of Asmara felt like stepping into a divine revelation. Asmara, a city of breath-taking beauty, once affectionately known as "Piccolo Roma" by the Italians, meaning "Little Rome," exudes a charm that is nothing short of celestial. According to UNESCO, Asmara is situated over 2,000 meters above sea level, Asmara has a rich history that dates far beyond the 1890s when it served as a military outpost for Italian colonial powers. In the 1930s, Asmara underwent a grand transformation with a construction program that embraced the Italian rationalist architectural style of the era. This led to the creation of stunning governmental buildings, residential and commercial structures, churches, mosques, synagogues, cinemas, hotels, and more, all of which contribute to the city's architectural splendour.

The cafes, cake shops, restaurants, and shopping opportunities in Asmara are nothing less than divine. Indeed, it can be a torturous experience to wander through its enchanting streets without money in your pockets, for the allure of its offerings is irresistible. Nevertheless, my sojourn in Asmara was a profoundly unique and enriching experience, a true testament to the city's divine beauty and cultural grandeur.

The training had begun, and I was commuting from Mr. Berhane's house to the hospital where my career training was taking place. It was conveniently within walking distance. From there, I was able to reconnect with other relatives and expand my network further. I couldn't contain my joy at having succeeded up to this point.

I am unable to adequately express my gratitude to everyone in my family and circle of friends who assisted me during my training. I was surprised by God's provision, ensuring I had adequate accommodation and food. It is said that "fortune favours the brave," and I like to think that my decision to take a risk was an act of bravery. For me, fortune came in the form of kind and generous people.

The generous support that I receive from Mrs. Meselesh and her daughter Lory, Mrs. Asefash Besirat's family, and Mr. Berhane's family is miraculous. These individuals have been like angels on earth to me. My good friend Tekue Retta Kassa offered to share his house with me. Tekue and I had attended the boarding school Adi-Quala together and shared a lot in common as he studied at a health assistant school. Thanks to their support, I truly enjoyed life in Asmara surrounded by so many wonderful people.

However, after a couple of months, something tragic occurred. I received the worst news of my life: my grandfather had passed away. This news reached me while I was attending the health assistant school. When my friend Nega shared the sorrowful news with me, I was overwhelmed with sadness and couldn't stop weeping.

When he passed away at the age of 84, he was truly a picture of vitality. Blessed with sharp mental acuity, a full head of hair, and teeth as strong as iron, he would boast that he could chew bones with ease. Though his sight and legs may have weakened with age, his overall strength and resilience remained unwavering. The connection I had with my grandfather was profound; he was the one person in my family whom I understood better than anyone else, so his passing hit me especially hard. I had dreamed of him being present at my graduation and witnessing my accomplishments in life. Sadly, I was unable to fulfil his hopes, which only added to the sorrow I was feeling. It was truly a devastating period for me.

I returned to Adi-Quala to mourn with my family, but I didn't see my brother Yosief. Unfortunately, he had joined the Eritrean People's Liberation Front (EPLF) with his friend. Yosief and his friend were honest, brave, and caring individuals who couldn't tolerate the injustices perpetrated by the 'Derg', the Ethiopian army. They fought for others with their bare hands. After many battles, a group of armed men shot them, leaving them for dead. Luckily, they survived their severe injuries. They were taken to a hospital and recovered, but they never returned home. When I heard this, I had mixed feelings: I was happy they survived, but deeply saddened that I couldn't see them. I thought he was shot by negligent behaviour, but I realised he had a deeper compassion for helpless people. He wanted to deliver them by his bare hand, and he paid the price. That visit marked the last time I went back to Adi-Quala and the boarding school. However, I hold onto the hope that I will revisit when the time is right.

Life in Asmara and studding my career was far more enjoyable and vibrant than my time at the boarding school. The training in the city granted me much more freedom and introduced me to a wider circle of friends and family, including the ever-helpful Samson and Yirgaw. My friend Nega was a true blessing; he was like a big brother to me, a mentor guiding me in spiritual life and ministry. He also introduced me to many friends and his family, frequently inviting me to join them for dinner. I admired him for his wit and knowledge. He was very popular, with many friends, and he often took me to new cafeterias where we enjoyed "fata," a popular traditional Eritrean meal.

Fata is a delicious and hearty dish made with a rich and spicy tomato, garlic, and onion sauce, soaked up with crusty bread and topped with natural yogurt. It remains a favourite among Eritreans. The dish was so filling and affordable that after eating fata, all you needed was to refill your water bottle. Following Nega's advice, you might not need to eat for the rest of the day. His clever suggestion was to add more salt to the dish, making us drink more water and eat less, thereby saving money.

Nega's humorous and resourceful nature made every meal an adventure. I fondly remember how we used to tease our acquaintance, who went to the cafeteria so often to order fata that the waiters stopped giving him menus and brought the dish straight to his table without even asking. Though we used to poke fun at him, I wonder where he is now and hope he is doing well in Eritrea. My friends Yirgaw and Samson, if you read this book by any chance, please get in touch. I love you. Those were the moments that made my time in Asmara truly unforgettable.

Sister Akberet Tekeste, the director of the Health Assistant School, provided me with shelter within the hospital along with other students. She even told me, "You are most welcome to dine with our family any time you want," knowing that I didn't have parents in Asmara. This act of kindness is encouraging and worth sharing around the world. I was surrounded by so many good people, and I will never forget this act of humanity. As she held firm beliefs as a Jehovah's Witness, I am uncertain of her current whereabouts. In 1994, the Eritrean government revoked the civil and political rights of Jehovah's Witnesses due to their stance on abstaining from voting in the referendum and from military service. I hope she is well with her family wherever she is.

After two years, Nega and I were almost finished with our training. One day, we were talking about the events that would take place on our graduation day. The graduation ceremony typically draws many guests who wish to share in the joyous occasion with the graduates. They bring flowers, and then the celebrations continue after everyone goes back to their houses. Nega was friendly with a lot of people and came from a big family, and so I knew he would have a great day. People will congratulate him with a bunch of flowers and post cards etc.

However, I didn't have anyone to join me in celebrating, so I found myself alone. As we prepared on the eve of graduation day, I joked to Nega, "I may just have to sneak into someone's garden tonight and snatch some flowers to put together a bouquet for a special someone. Maybe they'll return the favour with flowers for me on my big day. Can't have me being the only one flowerless at graduation!" My friend Nega laughed so hard and said, "That's a crazy idea."

"Your existence shouldn't be built on fear but on the solid foundation of self-assurance and bravery".

Luckily, three ladies named Yordanos, Fanus, and Gezachin, whom I knew from attending church services, presented me with some flowers and prepared a delicious dinner. They made it possible for me to celebrate my success with some of my closest friends, Kahsay. It was one of the best celebrations and a wonderful closure of my clueless adventure. Many generous people contributed to my career success. I am very grateful to them for that.

What I've learned is that life is often challenging, and it's easy to get stuck in repetitive cycles. When I felt trapped in a dead-end situation, I decided to take ownership of my future. Instead of waiting for others to decide my fate, I chose to be responsible for my own life. Navigating without guidance and clarity is not easy, but if I wanted my life to be different, I had to make it happen myself. Relying on luck or accidents to change my situation was not an option; I had to take action to avoid being stagnant.

Secondly, I understood the importance of exposing myself to new experiences and taking risks to improve my life. Risk is not inherently bad; it just needs to be well-assessed. By evaluating all options carefully, I realized that stepping out of my comfort zone was essential for growth. For example, moving from the orphanage to the capital city was risky, but it helped me develop a sense of responsibility. Life in the capital, along with God's provision and completing my career, boosted my confidence for future journeys. Though the journey may present challenges, I believe it will be worth it. Embrace the unknown, seize opportunities, and trust in your abilities. Your existence shouldn't be built on fear but on the solid foundation of self-assurance and bravery.

Lastly, planning and trusting in God should be the foundation of every step. The Bible instructs us to "trust in the LORD with all your heart and lean not on your own understanding; in all your ways acknowledge him, and he will direct your paths" (Proverbs 3:5-6). Relying on God is wise, but it doesn't mean being passive. We must learn to think clearly and make the most of every opportunity. Waiting for things to happen or for opportunities to fall into our laps can lead to missed chances. If I had relied solely on the director of the orphanage and waited for him to act on my behalf, I would still be waiting. Believing I was worthless, and incapable would have prevented me from becoming who I am today.

In essence, taking control of your future, embracing new experiences, and trusting in God's plan can transform your life. Embrace challenges, take risks, and have faith in yourself and be take ownership for your journey.

QUESTIONS AND SELF-REFLECTION FOR PRACTICAL STEPS

Question 1

What lessons have you learned from this chapter?

Question 2

What is the change(s) you want to see in your life presently?

Question 3

What principles or lessons will you apply to help you achieve the change(s)?

Question 4

Do you have a goal or vision for your life?

Question 5

What steps are you already taking to achieve it?

Question 6

Are there people for whom you are thankful for their presence in your life at some point? Name them and reach out to them where possible.

Chapter 3

DREAMS BEYOND MY CIRCUMSTANCES

Following the training that took place in Asmara, I was assigned to work in a medical facility in the city of Keren, which is 91 kilometres to the northwest of Asmara. My friend Mussie Gebeya and I were there for around six years and had a great experience with the people there. Mussie was very popular and nice person to me. The inhabitants of Keren are incredibly hospitable; throughout the time that I lived there my roommates and I would drink coffee together, and we would frequently pray and sing together. I started coming up with lyrics and melodies in my head and doing so delighted me.

My sister Luchia, wrote me a letter explaining how she had been struggling, having financial difficulties as well as the difficulties of living in Addis Ababa. I remember reading a particular passage that asked, "Why are we scattered over the ages? When are you and I going to catch up with one another? We don't get a fair chance in this life." While I was lying down on my bed and reading her letter, I found that I was unable to control the tears that were welling up in my eyes. I hid myself by covering my face with a pillow in case any of my roommates came home. After crying, I fell into a deep sleep for several hours.

My brother, who served in the military, had recently been discharged from active duty in the army. Even though I was the youngest, I had the distinct impression that the responsibility of needing to step in and assist was resting on my shoulders.

My first thought was to pack my bags and move to Addis Ababa, where I would establish a thriving medical practice and be able to support and care for my siblings. I took some time off from my job at Keren Hospital, and I also planned to borrow money from some family and close friends to fund the business plan. Then, right at the last minute, my friends backed out of their promise to lend me money. I remained in Asmara to find a way to help the situation, but unfortunately the clock was not on my side. The number of days that remained until I was required to report for duty in Keren decreased steadily as each new day passed. And the longer I remained in Asmara, the more I would spend the meagre amount of money that I had with me.

After some time had passed, I found myself with no money left. Feeling despondent, I sat down on the steps of a building in the middle of the city, questioning why everything seemed to be going so horribly wrong. The longer I sat there, I felt sorry for myself. As the sun beat down relentlessly, the heat became intolerable. I stood up to seek shade and felt someone standing behind me. Then, I began to hear a voice, repeatedly telling me that I was useless and incapable of helping anyone in any way.

In my thoughts, I kept hearing whispers that said, you could not provide support for your siblings. "It would be in your best interest to put an end to all your suffering. You would be better off dead because there is no reason for you to continue living." I briefly entertained the idea that it might be the solution to my problems. I was fortunate that it didn't take me long to regain my composure and choose to leave that place as soon as possible.

In the end, I made the decision to go back to Keren and carry on working in the hospital there. Even though the situation left me wounded and I was weighed down by the knowledge that I had not achieved my objectives, I came to the realisation that I needed to prioritise my life. Before I could help others, I needed to ensure that I was taking care of my own emotional and mental well-being first. After that, I made sure to cultivate a relationship with God by devoting time each day to prayer, worship, and the study of the Bible.

I have learned valuable lessons from my experiences, particularly when it comes to planning a business and relying on others. Borrowing money for a business from friends can have detrimental consequences, especially if the business does not succeed as expected. It can strain relationships with friends and family. I learned that it is better to avoid starting a business that heavily relies on friends. While seeking advice and collaborative help from them can be beneficial, it is best to approach a proper lender or a bank with a business plan. This approach provides a more stable foundation for the business and ensures that personal relationships remain intact.

Thankfully, my life was completely revitalised soon after this depressive episode. My roommates—Solomon, Getu, Afewerki, and Mussie—played an invaluable role in my recovery, as they surrounded me with prayers and songs during my time of need. Life in Keren, in the company of these remarkable friends, was truly invaluable. Together, we cultivated an atmosphere filled with laughter, joy, and profound meaning. Our lives were interwoven; we shared our rooms, meals, and a common purpose.

As our prayers with devoted pastors Amanuel, Mokenen, and Ghidey deepened, remarkable changes began to unfold within our prayer gatherings. I discovered an unravelling serenity and an infectious happiness blossoming within me. My anxiety dissipated entirely. It was in the midst of a heartfelt prayer that I found myself spontaneously bursting into song. In a ripple of harmony, everyone else joined in. The spontaneous joy of that moment surpassed all expectation, as such an experience was entirely new to me. I was overcome with astonishment and an exuberant joy.

Among the songs that I penned during that period was one that particularly resonated with us all, embodying the spirit of our shared journey and newfound happiness.

> *"I'm joyful, yes, joyful for being a Christian.*
> *I'm joyful because I'm born again.*
> *If I didn't find you, Jesus, where would I be?*
> *What would I look like?*
> *You have saved me by your grace.*
> *All my worry and misery are gone.*
> *I love you, my Lord.*

This song has sustained its popularity over the years, and to this day, many Pentecostal and evangelical believers affectionately know me as Daniel, the singer of 'I'm Joyful.' The song's enduring appeal was recorded on my first album.

I took comfort in knowing that both my daily activities as a Health Assistant at the hospital, and as a member of the congregation were both contributing to the greater good. During the time that I spent working at Keren Hospital, there was a nurse there who I had a crush on. Working as a Health Assistant at the young age of seventeen sometimes was boring or frustrating but having the chance to work in the same building as her was enough of an incentive for me. As we were friends, who not only worked together but attended the same church, sometimes she would invite me over to her house. In fact, this is where I met my friend Daniel Hagos Nashih for the first time.

My friend was someone who spent a lot of time in medical facilities. Anyone who knew nothing about him would probably automatically assume that he suffered from a debilitating illness that demanded on-going medical care, as he did not work at the hospital. The truth of the matter was, however, that he also had a crush on the same nurse as me. Over a while, he became a well-known figure at the medical facility, and we developed a close friendship. He invited me to his home and introduced me to the rest of his family, who are all precious to me. We developed a genuine and strong friendship and to this day, continue to be very good friends with one another.

His brother, Samuel, had settled in Sweden at the time. One time he came back to visit his family in Keren, and we were having a conversation about life in general when he asked me what I wanted to become. At the time, I didn't have a clear idea of what I wanted to do with my life. I shared with him my aspiration to pursue a career in singing but told him that I needed to own a guitar to accompany me in my musical endeavours. Samuel understood my passion and he was willing to send me a guitar with the help of another Swedish guy named Immanuel, and the two of them sent me a gorgeous 12-string guitar.

At this point in time, I was not yet familiar with how to play the guitar and had neither the time nor the additional funds to take lessons.

Because I wanted to sing while playing an instrument, I decided to teach myself how to play. I was able to accomplish this by spending a significant amount of time, typically anywhere from three to five hours per day, simply playing by ear.

I didn't get as much sleep as I needed to, but I made up for it with a lot of enthusiasm and determination to become a good player. Over time, I built up enough self-assurance to perform in front of my friends and even occasionally during our group Bible studies. I'm not claiming to be the best guitarist in the world but I'm happy that I'm able to accompany my own songs. The secret to having a successful life is to follow your passions. Discovering what you are most enthusiastic about is the most effective strategy for reaching your full potential.

Everyone aspires. Every one of us has a mental image of ourselves in the future, along with an idea of the kind of life we would like to live. The question is, "What does your mind picture? Are you willing to dream beyond your circumstances?" Well, I understand that for many, dreaming is futile and more of an escapist fantasy than a future possibility. It's important to dream, but it's also important to be realistic. However, dreaming doesn't have to be an unreachable goal. It can be as simple as having the audacity to try to move beyond your current situation.

Many people have the misconception that dreaming is a waste of time, but I believe that denying ourselves the opportunity to dream is more of a waste of time. Life can be difficult at times, and it can be very difficult if we only allow ourselves to focus on the problems. An important aspect that I consider adjacent to dreaming is meditating on what you appreciate in your life. In doing so, you sometimes find answers to your problems in the process.

I used to play songs of worship most of the time. Most of them were new and my own songs. When I did this, I would feel connected with something bigger than myself. A meaningful fellowship with God, the creator of the universe who holds everything, including the future. I felt inspired, healed, and captured by hope. I saw my problems beginning to fade away while simultaneously shifting my focus toward my dreams and visualising my future. I've benefited a lot from this experience, and it has become one of my favourite things to do, and I really love to do it over and over.

Because it gave me the ability to see a greater destiny, the knowledge that I could reach this destiny kept me going through all the struggles in my life. I would draw inspiration from my dreams. The most beautiful melodies would spring out of them, and I would feel the calming power of God and be in awe. The fog began to dissipate, which enabled me to think better and see more clearly so that I could visualise outside of my circumstances.

I've experienced two types of dreams. One is when you are asleep, and you see a series of images and occurrences that make no sense and don't necessarily have any meaning when you wake up. Usually, you forget what your dream was about, but other times, the dream is meaningful and significant enough to be remembered. The other kinds of dreams are our visions and desires that we aspire to be on a daily basis. We may not be able to see these kinds of dreams when we are asleep, but I think it is important to intentionally and consciously dream of something that is superior to and richer than whatever circumstance you are in right now. I believe that this is the key that will unlock your potential to stretch towards your destiny.

Helen Keller once said, "The only thing worse than being blind is having sight but no vision." Dreaming is one thing, but often people do not act towards achieving those dreams. There is no point in sitting around and wishing for something to happen unless you act on those wishes and strive to achieve them. During my childhood I used to be a daydreamer. I was able to see myself beyond the circumstances that had engulfed my existence. I would fantasise a lot, especially while I was sitting in a classroom, however it contributed to the inherent power I had to change the things that were going on around me. I believe it played a part in the life that I am able to enjoy now.

One of my dreams was to gather my siblings together and to have a beautiful family. To give hope and build a healthy community. I've seen my dreams achieved and hope that more will be accomplished in the future. For instance, to see my sister again, after such a long time, was like a dream come true. She had left Eritrea and gone to Addis

Ababa when I was young, so I didn't know very much about her. However, we were able to spend a lot of time together after we grew up. One of the best things about my time in Keren was that I invited my sister Luchia to come and live with us. Even though I couldn't go to Addis Ababa, she came to Keren and began to live with us.

Yosief, my older brother, would also come to stay with us from time to time, and it was incredible to have us all together again. Luchia, the kindest, happiest, and most generous person, delighted my friends with her delicious cooking. She was also exceptionally clean and tidy. We shared many memorable moments as family and friends. The combination of spending time with my siblings, having a job, and finally having a sense of purpose in life was an extraordinary experience. It felt as though I was being compensated for lost time, reclaiming precious moments with family that had been taken from me during my childhood.

My brother Yosief is a courageous, honest, and practical person who naturally captures the attention of others. Once, I introduced him to a cherished church family, and he ended up marrying their lovely daughter, Eden. They now have a beautiful family with two healthy children.

Life in Keren was filled with another level of fun and friendship, particularly with my friend Solomon. He often played the guitar for me while I practiced. Solomon was the funniest guy and was always straightforward. I recall the decision to celebrate my birthday, which was a significant moment for me. It was the first time I celebrated after discovering my birth certificate among my father's belongings during my grandfather's bereavement. Finding my birth certificate revealed my exact birth date, prompting me to start celebrating my birthday at the age of twenty-one. That year, I threw a party, cooked food, and invited friends over. Solomon, among the guests, noticed the "Happy 21st Birthday" banner and questioned my age. It must have surprised him that despite being nine years older, I had graduated from health assistance school before him.

My friends would encourage me to sing and practise playing the guitar, which led to a rapid improvement in my song writing abilities. My life in Keren was incredible. I had a solid community of family and friends around me, for what felt like the first time in my life. We would frequently go out to drink coffee and eat food together, and sometimes we would go out to play games like volleyball.

Recording My First Album

One of the full-time pastors, Pastor Amanuel Mokenen, who came from Asmara to preach, appreciated my songs, and he told me we needed to go to the mother church in Asmara to record my first album. He arranged for me to sing in front of a bigger congregation, and the church agreed to start the recording process in the church studio.

When I shared the news to a friend Eskindir Abed, he gave me the most important advice. He said that I should make sure to go for the best quality available because he had a terrible experience in the past where the sound quality of a recorded album was barely audible. So, I decided to do the recording in a professional recording studio.

The church studio was cramped, and it was basically a makeshift room that did not have any proper recording equipment. You had to sing very loudly in the hopes that the wind-up stereo recorder would pick up your vocals. There was a sign on the door that read, "Don't knock." The sign would be put up when the room was used for recording, but often people forgot to read the sign and would knock. Which then meant the take was ruined, and you had to start over from the beginning.

My decision to record in a professional studio was not received well by the congregation of the church, since it was secular and because it appeared as if I was looking down on the church's equipment. However, my intentions were only to make a better quality especially the lyrics should be audible and convey the message of the song to the hearers.

It took me a long time to find the best possible studio, but finally I found Admass Studio. I took my annual leave so that I could travel to Asmara. Typically, people would rent out the studio for days or weeks at a time, but I didn't have enough money for that, so I went ahead and asked the family who ran the studio if it was possible for us to prepare everything beforehand and then record it all in one day. I explained that I would not be receiving any money for this because it was just to share with the church community as a blessing. Mr Ghidey, the father who owned the studio, came out and he confirmed that it was possible to record my album within one day. I extended my annual leave to accommodate it, and I eventually went into the studio to record. The whole team prayed over the studio to sanctify it and run out any demons that may have been hiding. Natnael, Nahom and Yoel, Mr Ghidey's sons, all laughed when I told them this, but they thanked me. They were considerate and flexible people to accommodate my request.

The recording was beneficial to both the Full Gospel church and Admass Studio. The quality of the sound and music arrangement was exceptional, and the sale of the album supported the needs of the church. As a result of this success, I became a well-known gospel singer, attracting other singers to the studio looking to record their own music. In 1995, my first album was recorded and made available for distribution. The talented musicians who played a significant role in its creation: Kibrom, Lukas, Ghere, Essey, Heran, and Letina.

After recording my first album, the passion and prayer we engaged in inspired me towards a higher calling. The church in Keren city was growing, and I started experiencing special dreams, visions, and a burning passion to build community. The Eritrean Pentecostal Church was expanding and required full-time pastors who could plant churches and shepherd believers in various cities. So, I decided to pursue and achieve my dreams.

Preparing for a Higher Call

Working as a health assistant for more than six years was a deeply rewarding experience. The fellowship and network I created with the patients' families and witnessing the dramatic progress of the patients were incredibly fulfilling. However, despite the risks I took to get the job, I felt compelled to leave it when I sensed a greater purpose calling.

One morning, I decided not to return to my work anymore, and I never looked back. I went to Asmara for a short visit and was invited by a friend to participate in a spiritual program. During my time there, I encountered a prophecy that seemed directed at me: "I have called you for a higher purpose, separate yourself and be courageous." The next day, as I was meditating on this, I met my friend on Asmara's famous street, 'Combishtato, now Godena Harnet'. He was thrilled to see me and invited me to dinner, asking me to wait while he went to get a haircut. While I waited at a boutique I knew, I encountered two people. One of them greeted me warmly and, moments later, said, "Daniel, what are you waiting for? This is the time to minister to the Lord and build our community." I was speechless and astonished.

These messages resonated deeply with me, aligning with visions and dreams I had previously experienced. My heart was burning with passion to dedicate my time fully to ministry. However, I didn't feel spiritually ready, nor was I prepared to take the risk. Questions of residence, finances, and stability loomed large in my mind. The next day, I decided to return to my job. I bought a bus ticket and boarded the bus, but my heart was pounding, and I felt conflicted. I wondered if I was not trusting God and if I was hesitating in accepting the prophecy. I felt like Jonah, running away from God. Convinced that the bus might meet with misfortune because of my disobedience, I decided to get off and sold my ticket to someone else. At that moment, peace and overflowing joy filled my heart, and my mind settled.

Although there were still unanswered questions, I was confident and willing to pay the price.

A few weeks later, a lady named Elsa offered me her entire house in the heart of the city. She was going to Addis Ababa for an extended period. Her generous act greatly encouraged me and felt like a provision sent from above. I lived there for nearly a year while preparing for ministry and taking courses. Once I settled, I brought my personal belongings and bid farewell to my colleagues. A beloved brother, Joseph Alem, generously offered me his reliable and beautiful Jeep, which helped me move my belongings, including my cherished guitar—a special provision given the limited transport options.

My greatest challenge during that time was not having enough food. The longest stretch without food was four days, which I termed "forced fasting." One or two days without food became a norm, but those four days were particularly painful.

Despite these hardships, my schedule was quite busy. I ministered at every church I could and seized every opportunity to serve. By that time, I had become known as a solo singer, and my music encouraged many individuals.

While taking risks is crucial for personal growth and transformation, looking back, I recognize that I should have approached things differently.

In hindsight, I see that my decision-making process was flawed. I wish I had shared my passions, visions, dreams, and the prophecy I received with the church leaders to seek their guidance and clarity. Despite submitting a letter to the church leadership explaining my aspirations, shortcomings, and gifts, I received no response.

I realise that my communication with the church leadership and members was inadequate. I should have actively sought their thoughts and guidance, especially considering the impact on my well-being.

True leadership involves recognizing and nurturing people's potential to fulfil the church's mission. Unfortunately, the church leadership's actions were slow, and I felt unsupported and on the verge of burnout.

Looking back, I understand that I could have sought part-time work or explored other income-generating opportunities while awaiting the church's decision. My mindset at the time was limited, and I felt like I had to endure the situation alone, which was not the case.

Meaningful Fellowship

Meaningful fellowship is essential in our relationships with our brothers and sisters. While having many friends and being surrounded by people may seem like a blessing, it is truly the quality of the connections and the depth of the fellowship that truly matter. Fellowship should be meaningful, complimentary, and contributory. Each person has something unique to bring to the table, so shallow discussions will not lead to a meaningful fellowship. It is important to ask questions and seek understanding, even if we do not have all the answers at that moment.

I found myself surrounded by many people, but still feeling a sense of emptiness. Despite contributing my gifts to edify and uplift others, I still felt unfulfilled. Hearing the phrase "God bless you, brother" began to ring hollow when it was only said in passing.

When I share my experiences with others now, many express regrets that they were not able to contribute in a more meaningful way. This is why deep conversations should be intentional, especially among those in leadership positions or those who are mature and responsible.

Asking questions like, "Can you share your story with me? What are your biggest challenges? How can I support you?" can lead to more substantial and enriching conversations.

By fostering these deeper connections and engaging in meaningful dialogue, we can create a more supportive and fulfilling fellowship within our communities.

In 1997, while I was waiting, I managed to record my second album. After a few years, the Ghidey family expressed their gratitude, sharing that my album had been a blessing to them. Its popularity grew to the extent that singers would travel from Ethiopia to record at their studio. The studio even offered to assist me with my third album for free as a token of appreciation for bringing them numerous customers. Regrettably, circumstances forced me to flee to Sudan before taking them up on their generous offer.

The last time we crossed paths was in Sudan, where we were able to spend precious moments together. These memories will forever hold a special place in my heart, and I am filled with gratitude for the connection we shared.

Leadership Training

I have come to understand that effective church ministry necessitates proper training and qualification, especially in the areas of church planting and shepherding new members. Recognizing this need, the church I was associated with made the decision to send us to a Bible college led by the highly respected and honourable American couple, Jerry and Maxine Falley. Under their guidance, we received invaluable teachings and mentorship that greatly contributed to shaping us into better leaders.

Jerry, a tall and elegant man, is known for his punctuality, organisation skills, and strategic planning. Despite his serious demeanour and his appreciation for a disciplined life, he also has a humorous side; he often used to share entertaining stories with us. I recall when one of our classmates finally got engaged after many trials, we were all happy for him and celebrating when Jerry shook his hand and said, "Congratulations, and now the problems begin." We all burst into laughter.

On the other hand, Maxine exudes humility and quiet grace, her sparkling smile speaking volumes. Her wise teachings imparted with her gentle voice left a lasting impact on us. She emphasised the significance of negotiation skills within a family dynamic, offering valuable insights into maintaining harmony and communication.

One significant task assigned to us by Jerry was to document the number of churches in Eritrea. My best friend, John Alula, was entrusted with this important assignment, tasked with recording every church he could find in the major cities and towns across the country. Our journey took us to places beyond Asmara, such as Mendefera, Gindae,

Massawa, Dekemhare, and Adi Keyih, where we diligently documented the presence of churches in these locations.

It was a wonderful experience and we enjoyed spending time on the road, visiting new churches and exploring places we had never visited before. John went around making a collection of videos and photo albums of our road adventures, and at night I would play music for us which allowed me to significantly improve my playing and singing skills during that time.

Training under Mr. and Mrs. Falley was essential for our ministry at that time, and even now after leaving Eritrea. I remember one of the modules focused on cross-cultural ministry. They taught us to love our own people in Eritrea by studying and researching their cultures and identifying the kind of help they needed. Additionally, they prepared us for the future. Without their training, we would have been naive even in foreign lands.

After some training, I remember my first assignment as a minister of the church in the city Akurdet, in the western province. After a brief period, we went to establish a church in city called 'Tesseney', which is in the western part of Eritrea, close to the border with Sudan. John Russom, an amazing evangelist, was tasked with establishing a church in Tesseney and I accompanied him. Yonatan, a popular gospel singer, also joined us and we all had a great time together. Tesseney was very hot and sandy; one day I was making rice when I dropped the bowl of rice on the ground. We were really hungry and very impatient, so we decided to eat it anyway. The rice tasted nice, but the sand was gritty, and I managed to eat an entire spoonful of sand by accident, which caused me to choke and end up having a coughing fit. As a result of this experience, we learned never to put any food on the ground. We had a fun and productive time. Unfortunately, our dear friend John was killed in the 1998 border war, he laid down his precious life to protect his country.

Working in Massawa, which is a popular tourist destination with a very hot climate, was a very interesting experience. Many people would come to see the port, the Italian-style architecture, and to experience swimming on the beach. Although we would have a lot of visitors it was very expensive to welcome all of them properly. I remember letting my friend in on my strategy and he laughed when I told him about it. This allowed us to be polite without breaking the bank, as we would first offer them watermelon until they were full so that when we offered food, which we most likely didn't have enough of, they would be too full to accept.

I used to make regular trips to Asmara to visit friends and family. My friend John Alula often sought my assistance in mediating disputes within the church or among his circle of friends. Since I was not originally from Asmara, I approached these conflicts with impartiality, as I had no personal stake in them. I believe I had a good listening ear and the experience I gained from my time in the orphanage equipped me with the ability to act as a mediator when needed.

There was a notable occasion when an educated and older individual approached me seeking counselling. I felt nervous as I had never encountered such complex problems before. I listened attentively, silently praying for guidance to help address his concerns. As I began to speak, offering words of wisdom, I witnessed a remarkable transformation. His face lit up, and his spirit lifted. He expressed his gratitude by jumping up and embracing me. I realised that the wisdom that flowed through me was a divine gift from God.

After serving in Massawa, both churches I worked with experienced rapid growth. Unfortunately, in May 2002, the Eritrean government officially shut down Pentecostal and Evangelical churches, abruptly halting their progress.

The lessons I have gleaned from my ministry are both simple and profound. As David Young Cho appropriately expressed, "Visions and dreams are the language of the Holy Spirit." It holds true that without visions and dreams, true transformation is difficult to achieve. Therefore, my advice is to embrace and be inspired by the power of dreaming. Allow your mind to envision possibilities and transcend your current circumstances. When you place your trust in God and start small steps, I believe you will experience some transformation in your life. Starting with faith and taking some practical action, even in the smallest of ways, opens the door to new possibilities. As we embrace this journey, you may encounter challenges and uncertainties, but with God as our anchor, we can navigate through them. Trusting in God's timing and providence allows us to experience personal growth, spiritual development, and meaningful transformations that go beyond our own expectations

However, it is crucial to recognize potential obstacles that may arise when you seek to apply these dreams practically in your life. Negative self-perception, a detrimental attitude, and individuals or groups who discourage you from reaching your full potential can hinder your progress. For instance, consider the story of Joseph, known as the "king of dreams." When he shared his dreams with his brothers, they plotted to harm him and eventually sold him into slavery (Genesis 37).

Therefore, while dreams and visions fuel our aspirations, it is essential to navigate the challenges that may come our way. Surround yourself with supportive individuals, cultivate a positive mindset, and persevere despite the obstacles. By doing so, you can turn dreams into reality and fulfil the potential that lies within you.

If you don't think highly of your value or don't consider yourself worthy of anything good, then you won't be able to get very far in life. There is always a balance that needs to be found between self-hatred and narcissism. Be wary of pessimistic people because their words can drag your self-esteem down indirectly and unintentionally.

Working as a pastor and singer was just incredible; I was happy, busy and productive in my life. To me, it sounded like I was living my dreams. My ministry was growing, the church was advancing, I recorded my second album which I dedicated to the church. My influence and my gift were increasing. However, life in Eritrea started to be more difficult as there was another war breakout on a border dispute between Eritrea and Ethiopia.

What I have learned is that life can be a rollercoaster; however, it is your responsibility to keep going and be consistent. No matter how tough the situation, keep dreaming and moving forward. Be generous but wise to avoid being taken advantage of. Courage and discipline are crucial in turning dreams into reality. Don't hesitate to say "yes" to what you like and "no" to what you don't. Relying on God, mental, and spiritual strength is vital to achieving your vision.

QUESTIONS AND SELF-REFLECTION FOR PRACTICAL STEPS

Please take this opportunity to learn from the story and apply its lessons to your own life. Encourage and challenge yourself to think critically, dream big, and strive for positive change in the world. Your perspectives and experiences are unique, so embrace them and use them to make a difference.

Question 1

What lessons have you learned from this chapter?

Question 2

Do you have a dream(s) that keeps you awake? State it/them.

Question 3

How does it inspire your daily lifestyle?

Question 4

Can you identify obstacles (individuals, groups of people, environment, background, etc.) that could hinder the achievement of these dreams?

Question 5

How willing and committed are you to making your dream(s) come true?

Chapter 4

TURNING MY THREATS INTO OPPORTUNITIES

I remember when the Eritrean government decided to conscript civilians into the military by force. There were rampant roundups in different cities. I was in the port city of Massawa working as a community pastor. One day, at around five in the morning, I heard a loud banging on my door.

My initial thoughts were that it might have been a drunkard who had lost his way home. Upon opening the door, I wished it had been some-one intoxicated with liquor because the alternative that I found myself staring at was scary and unexpected. It was a group of armed military policemen carrying guns and batons, looking as intimidating as ever. One of the soldiers shouted, “Get out!”. I told him “I’m a pastor of the church”, to which he replied even more angrily, "I don’t care; get out now!" Realising that they weren’t going to leave without me, I asked to be allowed to change out of my pyjamas. He granted me two minutes to change, but I was not given any privacy.

A soldier accompanied me into the room, and there he found another person, a friend of mine who was visiting from Asmara. One of the soldiers told us, "Both of you follow me". He was taking us towards a small yard by the cinema venue in the city. We could see from a distance that there were many people who had been rounded up that morning to be conscripted into the army.

As we headed towards the group, the soldier's attention was distracted. He spotted another two people walking down the street, so he went over to inquire if they had permit papers that would exempt them from conscription. My friend seized that small window of opportunity to get away.

He jumped into a yellow taxi and asked the driver to get away from the area as fast as possible and drive him to Asmara. I was really tempted to go with him, but I couldn't because I was responsible for all the church's activities. Since our captors hadn't provided any explanation, I was also unsure of what was really going on. I was only hoping that once they knew who I was, they would let me go so I could return to my pastoral duties. After we waited a couple of hours, they took us to a big compound where they were holding thousands of other people that had been rounded up earlier. It was a very chaotic situation. There were people from all walks of life—professionals, labourers, high school students, and even some with mental health issues. In the afternoon, some of the organisations, such as hospitals, came to the compound to inquire about their members of staff as every critical task had been disrupted in their absence. Hospitals had been running at minimum capacity, unable to cater to patients' medical needs. There weren't enough professionals available to administer medication or perform surgeries on patients. Consequently, healthcare workers were released following an intervention from health officials. Being on high alert and seeking any opportunity to escape, I seized the moment as the healthcare workers began boarding vehicles. With the assistance of my friend Nega, who used to work at Massawa Hospital and was also a friend from high school in Adi-Quala, I managed to sneak into one of the vehicles. Determined to avoid forced conscription, I made the decision to leave the city and head towards Asmara.

I reported to our office in Asmara, but the mission director told me that I had to go back to Massawa even if there was a roundup. Even after explaining my situation about how I had fled the camp and how my life could be in danger if I was seen as a deserter for fleeing, he remained unmoved by my plight. "If you fail to return to your mission, we will have no other choice but to relieve you of your pastoral duties, and we will have to discontinue paying your salary." His lack of understanding of my situation deeply perplexed me. I decided to take my annual leave to buy time, pray about the situation, and plan how to go forward without affecting my calling. The more I thought and meditated about it, the more I felt the conviction to remain in Asmara, no matter the consequences. Quite frankly, it had been very challenging to get by without any regular income for about a month. I was back to my old lifestyle, eating humble fata. As the days went by, I realised I needed to venture out and find ways to earn a living to keep me going with minimal disruption to my ministry.

After a short period of time, I came up with a business idea to distribute food from wholesalers to local shop owners. The only problem was that I needed some capital to start the business. After a few weeks, my friend John Alula told me he had some money that he'd saved up for house rent. Johnny said I could borrow the money, provided I would be able to return it within a month in time for him to pay his rent. I gladly accepted the offer, and I was determined to ensure everything would go according to plan. Fortunately, within one month, I paid back all the money to my friend, and I had enough money to continue my business. I remember my first profit in one day being 250 nakfas, the currency used in Eritrea. That amounted to half of my entire month's salary at the church. I remember sitting down with another friend, called Efrem, to count how much profit I had made. I must confess that I was never good at mathematics or calculations. I had added an extra zero by mistake when calculating. My face was beaming with excitement at the thought of making 2,500 nakfas in one day, only for Efrem to bring me back down to earth with his hysterical laughter and point out the error. The business grew enormously within four months. Soon, I was involved in foreign currency exchange, buying, and selling video cameras, and continuing to supply and distribute foodstuffs.

This adventurous journey wouldn't have been possible without the support of a few friends, namely John, Isak, and Zeray. I am immensely grateful to Isak Bihon and his wonderful wife Sofia for their unwavering support throughout my business endeavours. They welcomed me into their home for dinner and even offered me a place to stay, creating countless cherished memories together. Despite the distance, we have remained in contact, and I had the pleasure of visiting them in San Jose, California.

I must also acknowledge the invaluable contribution of Zeray, a compassionate businessman who ran several successful ventures. His Christ-like character and generosity knew no bounds as he consistently encouraged my business growth. Zeray even went as far as offering his own vehicle to transport goods, which significantly aided in the expansion of my business. Their support and provision of resources played a crucial role in the success of my endeavours. Last year, during my visit to Dubai, I had the opportunity to surprise Zeray with a special dinner, expressing my gratitude and appreciation for his selfless deeds.

I really liked my job because it gave me the flexibility and creativity to think well. I was my own boss and that helped me set my own goals and visualise my dreams. The best part was that I had enough time to continue with my ministry and daily prayer time. I was invited to minister to the students' union at Asmara University. Many people were coming for a time of prayer and worship. One of them was Helen Berhane, now a very popular gospel singer. Helen used to come regularly to seek advice and grow her ministry. She was a very passionate and dedicated person. She truly had an anointing and was fearless in her public evangelism. Her boldness got her in trouble with the authorities, and she was arrested for many months and held in a shipping container. She eventually managed to escape and currently lives in Europe, where she wrote a book, "Nightingale" detailing the events of her story. She managed to contact me when she escaped Eritrea and we have kept in contact since.

After running a successful start-up business for almost six months I finally began to enjoy life in Asmara. I started dating the most beautiful girl in the world, Senayit. I met her a couple of years ago when I was counselling and reconciling conflicts. I remember I was invited to advise her on how her relationship could work with her fiancé, but unfortunately, it didn't work, and their relationship soon came to an end. After a couple of years, we started dating. My friend John and others used to make a joke, and they were suspicious as if I'd ruined their relationship. I used to jokingly answer back of course I did. But no, I didn't. In all honesty, during that time I was engaged to a beautiful lady. However, her parents didn't allow her to marry me. I'm not sure why but it could have been because of my choice of career, I was a community pastor, and my income was low compared to others. There is no big money in the church, especially in Eritrea. It could have also been due to the location of where I used to work. I was outside of Asmara most of the time. So there was a serious conflict between them and me. Finally, we decided to end the relationship mutually and amicably. Which worked out well for both of us.

Confinement in Asmara

Meeting Senayit brought me a great deal of comfort. We spent many hours talking, enjoying coffee, and dining at special restaurants serving traditional cuisine. To impress her, I even avoided eating fata, fearing it might spoil my engagement plans. We were meticulously planning our wedding day, and I was filled with unparalleled joy. With my business thriving and my ministry progressing smoothly, love was blossoming in our relationship. I often found myself thinking, "What more could I ask for?" Then, suddenly, the regime increased its patrols and began to arbitrarily round up people on the streets of Asmara. It became almost impossible to move around without specially issued mobility papers that proved one was exempt from joining the army.

The suddenness of these roundups caught everyone off guard. I vividly recall sitting in a coffee shop, engrossed in discussions about closing a business deal with my co-worker when the news reached me. It was then that my good friend, Mr DG, came to my rescue. He urgently informed me of the military police's presence and advised me to leave immediately and follow him to safety. We swiftly made our way to his car, where we observed the streets swarming with military personnel. Thanks to his quick thinking and connections, as he worked for a defence minister at the time, we were able to navigate away from the area without encountering any obstacles. Thankfully, we were never stopped for permit checks, and he safely dropped me off at my friend John Alula's apartment.

I will never forget his kind and thoughtful action to rescue me. May God reward him wherever he is.

I stayed there for about eight months. The good news is that I really enjoyed being with my best friend, John. He made sure that his sisters took very good care of me. His mother, a very strong woman, was in Europe to see his brother. I used to contribute towards the house rent and food expenses, so we were comfortable. We used to laugh, eat, and pray together. I had plenty of time to entertain him and the family. I sometimes used to make fun of him to deliberately annoy him. It was, of course, pure banter among friends. I remember one morning he dressed up to go to work. He usually wore a casual shirt and jeans, but that morning he put on a waistcoat on top of his shirt. He asked for my opinion. I think he wanted to impress some girls. Anyway, I said, "You look amazing, but it would be great if you took off the waist-coat." He insisted on putting on his waistcoat, and I asked, "Why?" He said it made him look more mature. "Doesn't the Bible teach us to be mature in our minds rather than in the way we dress? How long are you going to keep that look? You should focus on mature thinking instead of just looking the part" I said to him. "What do you know about how maturity?" John furiously exclaimed before storming out of the room. I couldn't contain myself and began to giggle. He returned to the room to see if I was winding him up. In between bursts of laughter, I told him I was, and we continued laughing together. John is a very generous, kind, honest and God-fearing person. I thank God for his loyal friendship.

Even though I had sought refuge in a loving home and my basic daily needs were met, it still wasn't easy being contained in a house 24/7. There was no way for me to get out of the house to meet other friends, go for a stroll and enjoy the sunshine, go shopping, or even go to the gym. Being confined and limited to a small space is awful.

I was so angry with the government that I refused to fight for many reasons. I was reminded of my childhood: all my suffering and how horrible it was growing up without love, protection or parents. The fatherly advice I had gone without because my father laid down his life to protect his country. As a pastor, I felt I should have been exempt from any military activity, just like all the other priests at the Orthodox and Catholic churches. I was entitled to be exempt because the law states that if your father is a martyr and your other siblings have been actively called up to fight in the war and you are the only male remaining from your household, you would be exempt. I qualified on all three grounds. I tried to raise my issue with government officials, but no one cared to listen.

I once approached Mr Z Yohannes, a senior government official. I had been informed in confidence by a friend that he was the key person to investigate my situation because he knew my father was a martyr. They used to know each other personally. I was optimistic and decided to write him a letter to be delivered in person. I was able to go to his office without a permit. I explained my situation clearly and that I was desperate for his help. I waited patiently for weeks, but I didn't get an answer. Finally, I decided to meet him face-to-face in case he didn't get time to read my letter. I found someone who knew his house and offered to drive me for safety and to avoid roundups.

I was dropped off at his magnificent villa and knocked on the door. His wife opened the door for me, and he was sitting in his beautiful living room with his son. I introduced my full name, and he asked me if I was the son of Habtey the martyr. I said, "Yes, sir." He told me to sit down. They were watching a James Bond film, and I joined them, but in all honesty, I was filled with mixed emotions. On one hand, there I was, meeting a high-ranking official who knew my father up close and in person. On the other hand, what if he had already read my letter but didn't like seeing me show up at his home unannounced? I was very nervous.

Then suddenly, he disappeared. I thought maybe he remembered my father, and he got emotional and went to the bathroom to wash his face. It had been about 15 minutes of anxious waiting since he left the room. I waited patiently for him to reappear, but the wait continued for what felt like eternity. His son was deeply immersed in the movie. I started to wonder what on earth was going on. A few moments later, another man emerged into the living room and asked Mr Zy's son to call his father. After disappearing momentarily, the boy returned. "My father told you to come inside," he told the waiting man. The man went into one of the rooms where, I can only assume, Mr Z was. Five minutes later, he exited the house with a wide smile and an air of happiness. It was clear that whatever concerns he had shared, he had received the answer he sought.

I was eagerly awaiting his call or his return to the living room. Another twenty long minutes passed before my frustrations became evident. Finally, I decided to approach his son and politely ask him if he could perhaps remind his father that I was still waiting for him. He relayed my message to his father and returned to where I had been sitting. " My father says he's not feeling well and that he will not be able to see you." He said, "You are free to leave." Overwhelmed with sheer disbelief and disappointment, I left his place feeling humiliated for the inhumane way he had handled the situation.

I had tried every possible way to be exempted, but it seemed that no one cared, not even the senior official who knew my father personally and had served alongside him in defending our country. However, unfortunately, my father didn't survive, whereas this officer did, yet it was evident that he failed to fulfil his duty.

I knew the government was corrupt for various reasons. For instance, I personally knew individuals who were exempt from military recruitment solely because of their connections with senior government officials and army officers.

All these pieces of evidence made me suspicious of their propaganda.

The Eritrean government accused the Ethiopian government of incursion, while the Ethiopian government claimed Eritrea had occupied a border area following clashes with Ethiopian security forces. Despite the challenges in determining the conflict's exact initiator, the Permanent Court of Arbitration, in its concise seven-page decision, found Eritrea guilty of violating Article 2(4) of the United Nations Charter by resorting to armed force on May 12, 1998, and subsequently occupying the town of 'Badme'.

Regardless of the initial aggressor, both countries suffered significant financial losses. As one observer aptly put it, "Two bald men fighting over a comb," capturing the absurdity of their conflict over a small, barren mountainous area where few people reside. This futile struggle resulted in tragic human losses, with tens of thousands losing their lives—a profound and irreplaceable loss for both nations. As the economist's analogy suggests, the conflict was ultimately senseless. Despite these sobering experiences, including those involving my own father, I find myself compelled to recount my story from a place of forced exile.

Joining the army seemed inconceivable to me, especially in a one-party system where there had been no elections since independence. The lack of democracy, freedom of speech, and religion, coupled with the absence of human rights, made it impossible for me to consider fighting for a country that didn't uphold these fundamental values. I had witnessed numerous individuals being arrested for their religious beliefs and political opinions, further solidifying my stance against the government's authoritarian rule. Despite the isolation I felt from the rest of the world, I remained steadfast in my decision, unwilling to compromise my principles for a system that oppressed its own people.

Sometimes, I would look through the window and see military police stopping and searching vehicles; they would stop people and ask them for a pass. If they failed to produce the necessary documents, they handcuffed them and took them away in a car. That was the first time I remember being afraid of a government that was supposed to protect and defend me. My father sacrificed his life for the freedom and liberty of the Eritrean people. Why did his son have to go through the feeling of being threatened and scared of the government?

The brutality of the Eritrean dictatorship is something one would find in horror books. It knows no bounds. In 1994, war-disabled veterans who lost limbs fighting for independence approached the government with the simple request of seeking improvements to their very basic living conditions. Instead of honouring them for their sacrifices, the government disposed of them by sending them off to a separate, dedicated camp in a place called "Mai Habar", located about 29 km from the capital city, segregated from the rest of society. Their persistent pleas fell on deaf ears until they decided to protest their squalid living conditions. The veterans, most of whom were wheelchair-bound, decided to head to Asmara to take their complaints straight to the seat of government. A special unit travelled to their location, and after a heated exchange of words, the defenceless army veterans were gunned down while in their wheelchairs because the government had zero tolerance for dissent. In a country governed by a single party system and with a solitary state-owned TV and radio station, the oppressive government of Isaias Afwerki pulled the strings to steer the narrative in any direction he so pleased. News of the massacre broke in the state-run Tigrinya newspaper "Hadas Eritrea" to the effect that "a disagreement that resulted in an altercation between a delegation sent over to mediate with the war veterans led to the unfortunate deaths of a small number of disabled military personnel." This incident happened just three years after the country became independent, when the euphoria of liberation had still not worn off among the public. While nobody had the courage to speak out, it was clear for all to see that this was a brutal regime in the making. This was not the promised "liberation" that the nation's fallen heroes had died for. If this is how the government mistreated its own war veterans who brought it to power, what chance did the rest of the civilian population have to survive under their iron grip of power?

It was with this knowledge of what the regime was capable of that I decided I wasn't going to be conscripted into the army. I had no other alternative but to hide in plain sight until I could figure out what my next move would be. Imagine living a life of fear and intimidation in your own country.

Even when sleeping, recurring nightmares dominated, which is a clear indication of post-traumatic stress disorder. During the daytime, you are constantly reminded of the precious lives perishing at the hands of merciless people in power—the very same people you thought were there to preserve life, not destroy it. It was an experience that fostered my paranoia, and I was constantly praying that I wouldn't get caught. Whenever I heard a knock at the door during the day, I always thought that they'd come to get me.

At night, any unusual sounds of footsteps, a vehicle stopping nearby, or anything and everything out of the ordinary sent my fears and anxiety into overdrive. No matter how much I tried to convince myself I was just hearing things, I could not refocus my attention to think of anything else other than the hallucination that they would break in at any minute and grab hold of me. Given that I was almost always by myself it was a terrifying situation. I began to meditate often to force myself to recognise that it was futile to be so stressed over a situation I could not control.

Lockdown is an emotional wilderness. Due to the COVID-19 pandemic, many people can relate to this feeling. It came with great distress and brought on detrimental mental health issues for many people. As a result, feelings of anxiety, depression and anger took hold. During the COVID-19 lockdown in the comfort of my home in West Yorkshire, England, I was reminded of my imprisonment back in Asmara.

Back then, I knew I was in the middle of a threatening situation. I knew the roundups could last much longer. I really didn't know what else to do, so I decided to invest in myself to become the person I aspired to be. I didn't want the setbacks to hold me back. I felt I had to turn the threats that faced me into opportunities by preparing myself for the future.

Even though I couldn't change the situation I was in because it was completely out of my control, I knew there was no power stopping me from changing my mind-set. Some of the things I did were read books that would encourage and edify my spirit, pray, and meditate consistently, and work out to maintain and improve physical well-being. As a result, I felt much calmer, and my faith was strong despite the fear and uncertain future that had surrounded me. I was physically fit and ready in case I had to prepare for another impromptu escape similar to what had happened in Massawa.

I remember a friend of mine coming to visit me using a fake permit pass. After we had spent some time chatting, praying, and singing, he complimented me on my spiritual and physical strength. It was a long and tough journey, but I managed it well for my own benefit.

Military Training in Sawa

After eight months in hiding, I'd had enough of being confined, and I decided to go to the local administration zone to solve my problem. I explained to them that I should be exempt from conscription as my father had died, but that didn't matter to them. They commanded me to go to Sawa, the military camp. It was much scarier than my lock-down, but after anticipating this for so long, it was almost a relief to finally be there. The training became extremely intensive, and it wasn't long before I realised that I no longer belonged to myself. I was no longer the owner of my life. I had become the property of the military.

When we arrived in Sawa, everything was different from what I was used to. You must obey every command from a superior. If someone tells you to sit, you sit down until someone tells you to stand. They gave us military uniforms that we had to wear at all times during training. As I was going to get changed, someone called my name. I turned around and saw a soldier I didn't recognise.

As he approached me, his smile grew bigger. I immediately remembered his smiling face—my friend Alemseged from Keren. Fikadu, a supporter of my music, served as the unit's leader. The camp was so hot and dry. We used to burn a lot of calories in the heat, and he would invite me to drink an ice-cold Coke, something that was a rarity at such a place unless, of course, someone knew you personally.

One night, I heard my name being called, "Daniel Habtey! Come out now!" I felt very nervous because I didn't know what to expect. It's very easy to find yourself in trouble without any justification or any reasons provided as to why. But to my relief, the man who called me to step out was a good friend of mine and a very talented musician who, in fact, played the musical arrangement for my second album. I was not completely sure whether to hug Yosief or not. I just wasn't totally sure about what was permissible and what wasn't. But it absolutely felt good to see a familiar face out there.

He took me to a different location to meet another officer who was his friend. Getting to the new location proved tricky for me as it was quite dark with poor visibility under the black evening sky. After our host invited me to sit down, he asked me how I was doing. Feeling very uneasy, I replied, "I'm doing good". He then continued, "Do you remember me?" My memory had failed to recognise the officer. While I continued to struggle with my thoughts, trying to figure out who he was, he had already moved on.

"Go ahead and sing a song," he commanded with a serious look on his face. Was this a trick? Was he trying to get me to sing so that I could get in trouble for it, perhaps? I wasn't in any mood to consider my options or the consequences that may follow. I decided to get on with singing one of my songs and get it over and done with. "Well done; you can go now" he casually remarked. As I made my way out, bewildered by what had just happened, he continued, "By the way, my name is Bahrenegash. I'm a fan of your songs."

A few days later, he came to visit me at my unit, and he treated me to a cold drink of Sprite. Fikadu and Bahrenegash were training officers and they spoiled me from time to time with a cold drink. I was grateful for their friendship, and they had made my time at the camp tolerable.

The training in Sawa was very difficult. There were no beds or mattresses for the cadets to sleep on. Everyone slept on the floor and there were hundreds all sleeping side by side in hangars. The food was mostly lentils diluted with plenty of water. I used to struggle with heartburn and stomach aches. We used to get up early in the morning, around 5 a.m., after the first whistle. Everybody would fall in line and there would be a head count. If anybody failed to show up for the head count, the consequences would be so severely brutal that you would not wish it upon your worst enemy.

I remember an incident once when two of our fellow army trainees from the same unit failed to attend the early morning line-up. The commanding officer went to the hangars, where he found them sleeping on the floor. They were punished severely, getting pushed around and kicked violently and indiscriminately, even though they pleaded that they had been feeling sick and were unable to train. After feeling disgusted and terrified by what I had witnessed, I vowed to myself that I would never miss a single day of training, no matter what happened.

The training session was incredibly intense, with our unit leader, Tes, showing exceptional enthusiasm and determination. His passion for excellence was evident in everything he did, making him a truly inspiring figure to follow.

One incident that really stood out was during a marching exercise when one cadet couldn't keep his head up. Tes immediately stepped in, showing no mercy in his efforts to correct the cadet's mistake. He resorted to using extreme measures like shoving a stick under the cadet's chin to force his head up straight. It was a humiliating experience for the cadet, who was then subjected to further punishment under the scorching sun for the remainder of the day.

The intense discipline and fear instilled by Tes among the cadets only fuelled our determination to excel. Despite sustaining a leg injury during the competition, I pushed through the pain, determined not to disappoint our unit leader.

In the end, all the hard work paid off as our unit emerged victorious in the marching competition. However, the toll it took on our bodies was evident, with injuries like mine worsening due to the relentless training regimen. The experience was both challenging and rewarding, leaving a lasting impression on all of us.

After two gruelling weeks of intense military training, the situation took a drastic turn as the war with Ethiopia escalated. The Ethiopian army had seized control of areas surrounding the city of Barantu, where our training base was located. Panic ensued as all trainees were abruptly evacuated from the military base in Sawa, likely to avoid potential airstrikes and further danger. The chaos and confusion were palpable as the commanders struggled to maintain order amidst the escalating crisis.

The following morning, we were ordered to carry boxes of food to a field, only to be then told to return to 'Sawa' to retrieve our personal belongings. As I made my way back to base, the searing pain in my legs from the rigorous training made it clear that I wouldn't be able to endure the journey again. Despite the urgency to leave, I had to make the difficult decision to stay behind, unable to join the others in their evacuation.

Three days passed with only a small group of us remaining at the camp, including my friend and me, both suffering from serious leg injuries sustained during training. It was apparent that some of those who stayed back may have been tasked with keeping a watchful eye on the camp and ensuring our safety during the chaos.

The uncertainty and tension in the air were as palpable as ever, creating a sense of unease and anticipation for what was to come. It would be naive to assume that all of us were there because we had been nursing various ailments. But one thing was for certain: peace and quiet had filled the atmosphere in a place that was mainly known for its endless commotion. My friend and I were certainly enjoying the serenity we had come to experience. Unfortunately, it wasn't meant to last. During the afternoon, four days after everybody had left, the camp came under aerial bombardment by Ethiopian fighter jets.

I have never experienced such intense fear in my entire life. The sheer terror of facing imminent death, not knowing if the next moment would be my last, was overwhelming. Just as we were trying to process the aftermath of the first bombing, news came that the fighter planes were returning for a second round of attacks on the camp. Panic set in as a soldier urgently directed us to seek refuge in the bunkers, knowing that our lives were on the line.

Amidst the chaos, a group of trainee soldiers who had initially claimed they couldn't walk suddenly found the strength to sprint to safety as if they were seasoned distance runners. It was truly a sight to behold, watching them move with a newfound agility and speed in the face of imminent danger. My friend, who had been nursing a leg injury all week, surprised me by leaving me behind and dashing off at lightning speed. His sudden burst of energy and swiftness left me in awe, making me question if even the world's fastest man could have matched his pace in that moment. It was a stark reminder of the extraordinary capabilities that can emerge when adrenaline and the instinct for survival take over.

Crossing the Border

Days later, as my leg slowly began to heal, I saw an opportunity amidst the chaos to escape from Sawa. I hesitated at the prospect of crossing the border, torn between the desire to be with my beautiful fiancée who I left behind and the uncertain future that lay ahead. However, I took comfort in the fact that I wasn't alone in this decision - my friend Biniam shared my resolve to escape, and together we clandestinely broke away from the crowd, setting out on our journey. Along the way, we encountered another man who was also seeking to leave, and together, we set our sights on Sudan, he was really a good person. The prospect of finally breaking free from 'Sawa' was a ray of hope in an otherwise dark situation. However, our lack of knowledge about the route to Sudan and how to cross the border left us treading cautiously, hiding during daylight hours to evade detection by border patrols.

Under cover of night, we trekked through the darkness, guided by little more than blind faith and whispered prayers, hoping that each step brought us closer to our destination. The distant sound of gunshots served as a haunting reminder of the conflict that had claimed the lives of my family members, including my brother and father. As we pressed on, every shot echoed like a grim countdown to my own potential demise, stirring fears of whether I, too, would meet a similar fate. Thoughts of the end of my family lineage weighed heavily on my mind, as the spectre of death loomed ominously in the shadows.

Approaching the Sudanese border, we understood the gravity of our situation and sought the assistance of an agent to guide us past both Eritrean government forces and Sudanese guerrilla fighters. His strict instructions - no talking, no coughing, and to watch his every gesture closely - underscored the perils of our escape. With bated breath and nerves on edge, we followed his lead through the treacherous night, straining to keep pace and remain undetected.

After a gruelling journey, we finally crossed into Sudan, a wave of relief washing over me as the weight of our escape lifted. The sense of liberation and accomplishment was beyond words as I reflected on the risks taken and sacrifices made to secure a new life. Despite the potential stigma attached to deserting the army, I stood firm in my resolve, knowing that this was a pivotal moment that had changed the course of my future for the better.

This life-altering journey has taught me invaluable lessons in resilience and perseverance in the face of adversity. Despite the myriad of challenges that life presents, each struggle carries the potential for growth and transformation. Throughout my odyssey, I faced daunting circumstances that tested my courage and resolve. In these moments of trial, I learned that succumbing to fear and worry only serves to compound issues, whereas turning to prayer, gratitude, and holistic preparation can pave the way towards resolution and peace.

Maintaining the right attitude, particularly in times of crisis, is paramount to emerging as a victor rather than a victim. While external forces may seek to intimidate or disempower, it is crucial to steadfastly resist succumbing to bitterness or stagnation, opting instead for a mind-set marked by positivity and resilience.

Your responses to challenges not only shape the outcomes of your experiences but also reveal the essence of who you are. By adopting a mentality of strength and growth, one can transmute life's tribulations into opportunities for personal enrichment and empowerment.

My path led me from a land that stifled my religious freedom to a newfound spiritual calling inspired by compassionate missionaries who introduced me to the love of Jesus. Embracing this profound encounter, I embraced the roles of pastor and gospel singer, driven by a deep-seated desire to extend hope and support to the downtrodden and marginalised individuals in my community.

A personal pact was forged to embody the principles of peace, reconciliation, and compassion, reaffirming my vocation as a pastor. Though it would have been simpler to comply with governmental directives and remain in the military, my unwavering faith underscored the importance of standing firm in my convictions. The path diverging from my faith would never be an option, as following the will of God remained my guiding light.

Nelson Mandela's words resonate deeply: "I learned that courage is not the absence of fear but the triumph over it." Rather than striving to eradicate fear entirely, our focus should be on transcending its paralysing hold on our lives. The pursuit of a meaningful existence in the face of fear is not only feasible but also admirable.

I have come to recognize that enduring hardship fosters resilience and introspection, providing invaluable opportunities for growth. Rather than wallowing in despair amidst challenges, embracing patience and fortitude can lead to personal evolution and triumph over adversity.

QUESTIONS AND SELF-REFLECTION FOR PRACTICAL STEPS

Question 1

What lessons have you learned from this chapter?

Question 2

Take a look within you. What abilities come naturally for you?

Question 3

What challenges around you get your attention the most?

Question 4

How can your abilities help solve the problem or challenge you have stated?

Question 5

What principles or lessons will you apply to help you overcome challenges?

Chapter 5

DEVELOPING A CONSTRUCTIVE CHARACTER

My experience in Sudan was characterised by a profound sense of abundance and relief, a stark contrast to the harsh realities I faced in Eritrea. The Ethiopian army's air strike was a harrowing ordeal, and my brief stint in the training camp was equally disturbing. The relentless sound of gunfire was bewildering, adding to the chaos and fear that surrounded me. Crossing the border was an intensely frightening and perilous endeavour, a journey fraught with danger at every step. Despite these challenges, the relief I felt upon reaching Sudan was immense, a beacon of hope amidst the turmoil.

The following day, we were transported to a refugee camp named 'Gulsa'. Despite the camp's chaotic conditions and the scarcity of essentials such as food and water, I found solace in the camaraderie shared with my friends and fellow Eritreans who had undergone the arduous journey alongside me. While we were permitted to venture into nearby villages in search of sustenance, our funds began to dwindle after just a few days. Amidst the challenges and the looming uncertainty of our future, we discovered moments of unity and support amidst the adversities. As time passed, we devised a plan to journey to the nearest city in a quest to enhance our communication channels and secure additional resources.

During a critical juncture when the hardships at the camp peaked, a group of us clandestinely set out to break free and make our way to a telephone centre and other vital facilities. However, our pursuit was abruptly halted a few miles into our journey towards the bustling city of 'Kassala' by civil security officers. Their swift intervention, marked by aggressive commands and the unsettling display of firearms, compelled us to halt our advancement and ultimately led to us being apprehended and escorted back to the camp in custody.

Despite facing setbacks, my steadfast friend Biniam and I remained resolute in our determination to reach Kassala, while some of our companions opted to remain within the confines of the camp. The yearning to reconnect with my fiancé, Senayit, consumed me, prompting me to cling onto a small pocket mirror that held her image - a precious keepsake she had entrusted to me before my departure to the military camp. Biniam, with his infectious laughter and unwavering positivity, served as a beacon of hope, lightening our spirits even during the darkest of moments.

Upon finally arriving in Kassala, my immediate impulse was to contact Senayit in Asmara. Though relieved to know of my safety, a palpable sense of uncertainty tinged her voice as she grappled with the complexities of our impending reunion. As I bid her farewell over the phone, an amalgam of emotions intertwined within me, echoing the tumultuous journey that lay ahead.

Arriving in a new country with little to no knowledge of the language and culture is naturally quite challenging, as it forces you to rely heavily on the local system and the kindness of strangers. However, in my experience, the people of Sudan displayed remarkable kindness and generosity. Nonetheless, my friend and I made the decision to travel to the capital, Khartoum, as it seemed a safer option compared to Kassala, which bordered Eritrea. Additionally, Khartoum boasted a larger Eritrean community and better telephone connections, making it the preferred destination for us to reach out to our relatives abroad.

However, reaching Khartoum presented us with a couple of obstacles. Firstly, we lacked the necessary permit papers to move freely, and secondly, we were short on cash for transportation. Though I had some money, it wasn't enough to cover both of us, and I couldn't bear to leave my friend behind. In a moment of desperation, I remembered the precious necklace my fiancée had given me. Unsure of its value, I suggested selling it to fund our journey. At the jeweller's shop, we learned that the amount offered wouldn't suffice. Seeing our distress, the shop owner intervened with unexpected kindness. "You know what?" he said, his tone filled with compassion. "I'll provide you with all the money you need, and you can repay me whenever you're able." His generosity rendered us speechless. I'll never forget his warm heart and genuine smile. His act of kindness solidified my admiration for the people of Sudan, who welcomed us with open arms. With his blessing, we embarked on our journey to the bustling city of Khartoum.

Arriving in the capital was confusing. We didn't know where to go or who to ask for help. Our plan was to get away from home and find safety, but we didn't have a clear idea of where to go. Luckily, we met another person from Eritrea who showed us around Khartoum. With his help, we found a cheap hotel to stay in for a short time. But when we ran out of money, we had to sleep on the streets.

Luckily, the warm weather in Sudan made sleeping outside bearable. Since we didn't have money from abroad, I had to rely on my friend's connections for help, but it took a while to get any assistance. Eventually, we found refuge with people we knew, especially a friend from my past, Pastor Yohannes. Reconnecting with him was a huge relief. He and his church community were so kind, giving us food, shelter, and friendship. My friend Biniam also took care of me when he was in a better financial situation. I'm truly grateful for his kindness.

Staying with Pastor Yohannes and colleagues like Michael 'Hagele' made us feel a sense of belonging, even though we were far from home. The church members welcomed us warmly, inviting us to meals and events. Although I became known as a gospel singer, their kindness extended beyond any fame I had. However, when I received opportunities to minister at other churches, it caused tension within the local church due to misunderstandings. I tried to reconcile, but it was beyond my capacity.

Eventually, I had to choose either to remain without a ministry at the other church or to minister there and leave the first church. Deciding to leave was particularly hard because the church members were so kind. It was tough to navigate the conflicts, but I chose to follow what I felt was right. Even though it caused some sadness, I will always remember the support and friendship I found with Pastor Yohannes and his church. Michael 'Hagele' was a funny, loving, and caring person.

My Wedding Ceremony

After six months, my beautiful fiancée Senayit arrived in Khartoum. Fortunately, she didn't have to cross the border like I did; she flew directly from Asmara to Khartoum. My friend Bereket Yohannes accompanied me to welcome her at the airport.

There was a bit of drama upon her arrival; unfortunately, her luggage was mistakenly sent to London, as the plane was a transit flight. She struggled to find any spare clothes and had to borrow from friends. Despite this small inconvenience, it was nothing compared to crossing the border. After two weeks, her luggage finally arrived in Khartoum from London. I like to think it was a prophetic sign that our destination would be the UK.

I was overjoyed to see her again, as I had been eagerly looking forward to our reunion. Senayit is such a wonderful person—quiet yet wise, and beautiful both inside and out. Her character is truly admirable, and I couldn't wait for us to be joined under God.

Finally, we got married on January 13, 2001. It was one of the best days of my life. The sun was shining, the birds were singing, and I was overjoyed. Senayit looked absolutely gorgeous in her wedding dress. I wore a white and cream suit borrowed from my friend, Pastor Aklilu. Though the suit was a bit big for me, it suited me well, and I had no other option as I didn't have enough money to buy a new one.

When it came time to exchange vows, the church was full of people. I remember two different churches, Niftalem and Bethel, united just in time for our wedding. The priest was Ethiopian, the preacher was from Finland, and the choir was from Eritrea, making it feel like an international assembly. One of the church elders, Girma, who was leading the program, announced that the groom would now sing for everyone. As people clapped and cheered, he mentioned that most grooms are shy, but not this one.

The congregation laughed. I stepped out onto the stage; I was as equally nervous as I was excited, but I focused on gripping my guitar and strumming my favourite chords. The act of playing a melody calmed me and I began to sing. As I sang, I remember being in awe. I just couldn't believe that I was married in Sudan to the most beautiful woman in the world. I remembered God's mercy and protection over my journey, and I was moved. Suddenly the atmosphere was electric, and people were touched deeply; some were crying tears of joy, some gave out a shout of triumph, and some expressed their joy by ululating. It was simply amazing! I was over the moon. It was perhaps the second-best day of my life, only surpassed by the day I received the deliverance of my salvation.

The cutting of our wedding cake marked the beginning of the end of the ceremony. A wonderful couple named Daniel and Mekdes paid for the stunning cake and refreshments. I was full of gratitude for their generosity and that of everyone who made our big day colourful. I couldn't have asked for more; blessed be the name of the Lord! Afterwards many of the church members and guests told us that they'd never seen such a blessed wedding, and for some reason, this gave us a lot of favour and respect.

A wedding can be difficult without family and friends, especially for my wife, but we were incredibly fortunate to have friends there to support us. We received many lunch invitations for a couple of weeks afterward. Our honeymoon was full of memories, thanks to the help of friends, especially Fanus, Aklilu, Rihisty and Ariam. Even though we were in a strange land, God's blessings and kindness followed us.

Senayit is the most wonderful wife I could ever wish for—wise, patient, and brave. Together, we have navigated numerous perilous situations, yet we laughed through it all and continue to find joy and laughter in each other every day.

Throughout my journey, I have been privileged to encounter a diverse array of individuals in various capacities. Some wielded significant power and influence, including financial resources, yet they often misused their positions. Conversely, I have met people with modest power and positions who utilised their influence for greater purposes. The moments I shared with these individuals and their impact on my life are unforgettable. I have been deeply attracted, influenced, and challenged by them. I discovered that character is immensely powerful, perhaps the most influential force in shaping one's lifestyle, even amidst darkness.

Reflecting on the past fifty years of my life, I have observed that many people who once had power, money, and position are no longer in the same roles. Some have passed away without leaving a significant legacy, while others remain, but their reputations have suffered. In contrast, those with strong character have left a lasting impact, inspiring many others to follow in their footsteps. Their names will be remembered forever, and their rewards are even greater.

Perhaps this is one of the reasons I am writing this book—their true character continues to shine brightly in my life. The actions of these individuals in demonstrating humanity and leadership are outstanding. Among the many lessons life has taught me, one truth resonates profoundly: the immeasurable value of those who exemplify unwavering character. Their generosity, selflessness, and compassion during life's most trying moments stand out. I have witnessed people who set their lives as good examples in times of crisis. These noble souls extend their kindness and support freely, devoid of expectation or agenda, embodying genuine empathy and unwavering integrity. Their actions speak volumes, providing comfort and respect even in the darkest times.

The significance of such encounters cannot be overstated; they are timeless reminders of the transformative power of kindness and the enduring impact of authentic human connection. What I've learned is that everything else might fade, but true character leaves a deep and lasting influence. Money, fame, and other superficial achievements are quickly forgotten, but the influence of people with true character remains forever.

Navigating unfamiliar territory and embarking on new beginnings is not easy, and I must admit that I didn't always live up to my own standards. Whether succumbing to fear, allowing anger to overpower me, or grappling with feelings of jealousy and forgiveness, I faced my own shortcomings while exploring my identity. While there are aspects of my life that I'm proud of, I also acknowledge moments when I wish I had acted differently.

Life in Sudan brought new beginnings in many ways. It was my first time living outside my homeland, stepping out of my comfort zone and into new environments, experiencing cross-cultural exchanges. I was a newlywed, navigating the complexities of husband hood and fatherhood. In hindsight, it was a perfect laboratory for testing character, pushing me beyond familiar boundaries and revealing both strengths and weaknesses in equal measure. It's said that true character is revealed not in moments of ease but in the crucible of adversity. Sudan, with its blend of joyful celebration and profound challenge, was such a crucible.

As someone once remarked, "Character is not made in a crisis; it's revealed." It is true that in some ways, I was not happy with how my character was revealed during times of crisis. Especially when I felt abandoned by those I once called friends, it was a painful experience that inflicted emotional wounds. When fear and anger get the best of you, when there is no backup plan, and when you are responsible for taking care of others and things get complicated, these are perhaps the most critical times for testing character. Would you stick to your standards and values or react according to the situation? Would you handle the situation with good character?

There was a time when I was so angry and jealous of my friends and struggled to forgive. When I look back now, I realise I could have responded better because character is defined by doing good things even in the most difficult times. It is a self-imposed choice to maintain it even when it doesn't feel natural.

Character describes your lifestyle, whether it is in public or private, whereas personality describes your gifts, type, and talent inclinations. Many people have great personalities, but they may lack good character. To know a person's character, you must test their weaknesses. There is a difference between character and personality.

I believe personality is innate, something you are born with. It is a natural gift, an inclination, and the way you act. Personality is a mix of your inherited genes and upbringing, a result of both nature and nurture. While it can be slightly polished or influenced in your early stages by parents, surroundings, and culture, you cannot choose or change it greatly. There is no right or wrong in personality; it is just the way you are created, like traits like colour or gender. For example, I have three children, and each of them is completely different. They grew up in the same house, raised by the same parents with the same love and nurture, yet they have different personalities. Some are bubbly and sociable with extroverted personalities, whereas others are less sociable and more introverted.

Whereas character is something you choose, it embodies clear notions of right and wrong. Unlike personality, which is largely innate and influenced by genetics and early upbringing, character is shaped by your decisions and actions. Even though your associates might influence it, it can be consciously changed and developed, regardless of your surroundings and personality traits. As the Bible says, "Bad company corrupts good character" (1 Cor. 15:33).

Building character involves making ethical choices, demonstrating integrity, and adhering to moral principles, even when it's difficult. For example, you might choose to act with honesty in a situation where deceit would be easier or show kindness and forgiveness even when you feel wronged. These choices, repeated over time, strengthen your character.

Furthermore, character development is an on-going process. It requires self-reflection, learning from past mistakes, and a commitment to personal growth. No matter your starting point, you have the capacity to cultivate virtues such as courage, compassion, and perseverance, which define strong character. This journey of character building is accessible to everyone, regardless of their inherent personality traits.

In Khartoum, there was a small Ethiopian and Eritrean community church called 'Niftalem International Church'. The congregation was made up of people who were very welcoming. They wanted me to minister to them so badly that I joined them, even though it meant leaving the other church that had initially accepted me. I used to lead worship and sometimes train the choir, and often I would give pastoral care to the lead pastor. In the beginning, the pastor who was in charge liked my worship style and my counselling. He once made a promise to me saying that I would become the lead pastor if he ever left Sudan. Over the next couple of months many full-time pastors arrived from Eritrea and there was a lot of competition in the church.

The church was growing due to a massive influx of new arrivals from Eritrea. I remember when I first arrived there was a small congregation, and the church gathering was in a residential house. But gradually over about a year, as the numbers increased, we needed a bigger church building. We approached a friend and a teacher from America who helped us use the Khartoum Christian Centre (KCC). It was a great help and much appreciated by the leaders. Unfortunately, a leadership rivalry began to unravel among some of the elders and an unhealthy competition led to the disintegration of the church.

Struggling with Forgiveness

As far as I know, the conflict began just after my honeymoon, and it had been lingering for a long time due to various reasons. I might be wrong, but here is what I know. The senior pastor was in the process of leaving the church for a theological seminary in the USA. There was a need for another pastor to fill the vacant position and there were many full-time pastors who were ready to take over.

From what I gathered, there seemed to be some underlying tensions among the full-time ministers regarding the selection of the next leader. During a routine Bible study meeting, which happened to be my initial one following my honeymoon, I sensed strong criticism among the leaders and that created a dull atmosphere. One morning, one of the elders invited us for a conversation in the absence of the senior pastor.

The topic was how to make the church a better place. I said, "It all begins with leaders. We have many full-time pastors here, but we lack coordination. We need a clear job description for better productivity." I don't remember any comments from others, but most of them were quiet and we started to discuss what I'd said. The lead pastor called an emergency meeting the following day. Without any warning or explanation given, he said, "Daniel Habtey, you are no longer part of the leadership." I was shocked by the decision because I hadn't seen it coming.

The conflict that surfaced shortly after my honeymoon had been brewing beneath the surface for some time, driven by a variety of underlying tensions. As the weeks passed, the atmosphere during our regular leaders' Bible study meetings became increasingly strained, filled with critiques and an unsettling sense of unease.

Following my abrupt dismissal from the leadership team, I found myself grappling with a deep-seated sense of betrayal and disillusionment. The rift that emerged distanced me from individuals whom I had once regarded as close friends, plunging me into a tumultuous period characterised by emotional turmoil. As the first person to join the church, with many others following through my referrals, navigating this challenging situation proved particularly daunting.

Despite the lead pastor's eventual apology for his actions, the fallout from broken promises and unexplained decisions continued to weigh heavily on my mind.

Struggling with Jealousy

In Khartoum, the house we rented was conveniently located near the church chapel, making it a popular spot for social gatherings. Friends would often stop by before or after prayer meetings, creating a vibrant atmosphere in our home. Some of these friends seemed to lead a more privileged lifestyle than mine, despite arriving in the country after me. Their ability to afford luxuries that I couldn't obtain due to lack of job and financial support from overseas relatives left me feeling envious and insecure. I really hesitated if my life will be changed at all. These negative emotions began to weigh heavily on me, especially with my wife pregnant and the pressures of what happened in the church leadership amplifying my feelings of inadequacy.

However, I soon recognized that dwelling on jealousy, resentment and comparing myself to others was detrimental to my well-being. I knew I needed to shift my focus towards gratitude and contentment, rather than fixating on what I lacked in comparison to others. It became clear to me that I needed to confront these toxic emotions and reassess my perspective on my own blessings in life. Prideful displays of wealth from some individuals only worsened the situation, prompting me to take a step back and re-evaluate my priorities.

This change in mind-set brought a sense of empowerment and purpose to my life. As a result, I began to appreciate the good things in my life and count my blessings. Taking responsibility for my own happiness enabled me to move forward with confidence and determination. I learned that forgiveness is also a key component in finding peace and moving past difficult situations. By letting go of resentment and grudges, I was able to free myself from negative emotions and focus on a brighter future.

Struggling with Knowledge

Upon my arrival in Sudan, I was not proficient in the Arabic language, but I quickly realised the importance of learning it through interacting with locals. By making an effort to converse with Sudanese people and fostering positive relationships with them, I was able to pick up the language more rapidly. The friendly and welcoming nature of the Sudanese community played a crucial role in my language acquisition journey, as their willingness to engage and help me understand Arabic made the learning process much smoother.

Building wonderful relationships with the locals in Sudan not only enriched my cultural experience but also served as a valuable tool for language learning. Through regular interactions and conversations with Sudanese individuals, I was able to immerse myself in the language and practise it in real-life situations. Inviting people for traditional coffee ceremonies, a common social practice in Sudan, provided me with opportunities to engage in meaningful conversations, learn new vocabulary, and deepen my understanding of the language in a natural and authentic setting.

By embracing the language and forming positive connections with the local community, I not only improved my Arabic skills but also gained a deeper appreciation for Sudanese culture. The importance of language in fostering meaningful relationships cannot be overstated, as it serves as a bridge that connects people from different backgrounds and allows for genuine communication and understanding. Through my wonderful relationship with the local people in Sudan, I was able to navigate daily life more effectively, expand my cultural horizons, and establish a sense of belonging in my new environment.

Coffee ceremonies are a big part of Eritrean culture. It is common at all kinds of social gatherings, such as weddings, birthdays, and when you invite guests over. It makes people feel at home and relaxed. It is one of my favourite cultural ceremonies.

It encourages people to talk and get to know one another better because the coffee ceremony goes through three different stages, which gives everyone involved sufficient time to catch up. The aroma of the coffee and the atmosphere it creates is an experience of a lifetime. Even after moving to the UK, we still hold traditional coffee ceremonies at home to this day and invite our western friends to what would feel like an authentically exotic experience for them.

Some people, sometimes, complain about how long the ceremony takes and how it's just a waste of time. Others absolutely love it, including our children. In fact, they sometimes encourage us to make it if they see us looking bored. But for me and for my wife, it is more than just a routine exercise, it's when we sit down and discuss things, make serious decisions, and solve difficult issues over some coffee ceremonies.

Despite my best efforts, securing a job opportunity had proven to be quite challenging for me. Fortunately, my wife was able to secure a job, as it seemed easier for women to find work compared to men in the area. Even so, I was determined to find a way to contribute and support my wife, especially since she was pregnant at the time. I was adamant about being the one to care for her and meet her needs, rather than relying on her to provide for us.

After months of persistence, my language skills had significantly improved, allowing me to establish meaningful connections within the community. It was through these connections that I identified a demand for rental properties in the area. I reached out to an American friend of mine who had a strong network and asked him to refer anyone in need of renting a house to me so that I could act as their broker. He graciously agreed to assist me and would inform me whenever families were looking for rental properties, enabling me to help them find a suitable home.

Through dedication and networking, I was able to contribute to our household income by facilitating the rental process for families in need of housing. This not only provided me with a means of supporting my wife during her pregnancy but also allowed me to utilise my improved language skills and connections to help others in the community. By seizing this opportunity and taking an entrepreneurial approach, I was able to turn a challenging situation into a mutually beneficial arrangement for both myself and those in need of housing solutions.

I was excited about my new job and sought the assistance of my friend, Medhanie, who is fluent in Arabic. Medhanie is truly exceptionally humble, handsome, and, most importantly, incredibly loyal, and positive towards others. An American teacher informed me about a US family looking for a rental property. Medhanie and I set out on a quest, visiting every potential property we could find. We approached landlords and homeowners to gauge their interest in renting out their properties.

Ultimately, it was someone else who successfully found a home for the family. Our efforts had been futile. We spent days searching for available properties, hoping to secure at least one deal. However, we went months without any success. Medhanie grew increasingly frustrated and eventually decided to step back, leaving me to continue my own. He believed our efforts were not yielding results. I persevered with my improved Arabic language skills, resorting to hand gestures, and even switching to English when needed.

Eventually, my persistence paid off. A few months later, I remained determined to finalise a deal and successfully made it happen. I earned a few hundred dollars for my dedication, which meant the world to my wife and I. I invited my friend Medhanie to dinner and gave him a portion of the money as a token of appreciation for his previous assistance. He was amazed that I had managed to close the deal. As I continued in this job, my Arabic skills improved significantly, and my relationship with the locals flourished.

The Challenges of Parenting

Amidst the chaos of trying to make life work in Sudan my wife and I went through a completely new experience that would change our lives forever. We welcomed a baby girl, our firstborn. She brought so much joy into my life, but I can't say I wasn't scared to be a parent. I didn't know how to be a father. I didn't have one growing up and I was worried I would fail her. But as soon as she was born, I held her and looked into her eyes, and I knew I would do absolutely everything I could to make sure she had the safest, most privileged life I could give her.

Abseri was born in the hospital, and I was able to enter the delivery room and be there to witness her arrival in the world. It is not permitted in Sudan, but I managed to convince the nurse that they could benefit from my presence there because my wife did not speak any Arabic and I also used to be a health assistant. I showed her my ID, which was written in Tigrinya and Arabic, and she allowed me in. My wife was relieved, and I helped the nurses with interpreting for them and my wife. I welcomed our first child into my arms. What a moment it was! What a heavenly gift—so beautiful and adorable!

My life changed forever in that instant. Nothing ever prepares you for parenthood. I was now responsible for the life of another being. When our little girl was about four months old, I saw her flash a beautiful smile for the first time. It was the most beautiful thing I had ever seen. From then on, I used to rush home just to see her and make her laugh and smile. Sometimes she would already be asleep by the time I got home. I would wake her up by tickling her just to see her smile. It was a joy and a blessing to have a child. It was also a privilege to be a father. I do not think any words can describe the feeling of gratitude and appreciation one gets to experience as a parent.

In a strange twist of fate relations between Sudan and Eritrea became strained. The police, therefore, started cracking down on migrants, mainly hunting down Eritreans. Many were getting arrested and there was genuine fear that Khartoum would begin to deport them back to Eritrea. My wife and I had a habit of going out for a casual stroll and grabbing coffee mostly in the evening hours. We were only a few yards away from our home one evening. I was holding our baby girl as we walked when, suddenly, three soldiers came from behind and subdued me. One of them grabbed me by the neck. They were very loud and incredibly aggressive. They ordered me to hand my daughter over to her mother. No further explanation was given. My wife was utterly shocked, in tears and trembling. Then they put me in a car, drove off and threw me behind bars. Three days had gone by before anyone explained the reasons behind my imprisonment. I had been accused of helping someone leave the country illegally.

Finally, I was released on bail. There was a language barrier, and we didn't have any residence permits, which was nerve-racking. My wife was distraught by what had happened. She had been under the impression it had something to do with developments in deteriorating political relations. Her biggest fear was that they would deport me back to Eritrea, which would have effectively marked the end of my life.

Immediately after my release, my wife decided that we should leave the country. She has been planning this while I was in prison with the assistance of our friends, Kaleb and Tes, So, she arranged for us to travel to Libya through the Sahara Desert. The generosity and support of these two friends were incredible, and I will never forget their unwavering presence during our darkest times. I was amazed by my wife's brave decision, considering our baby girl was only six months old at the time. However, the tragic stories of refugees embarking on the perilous journey and losing their lives along the way made me hesitate.

It took quite some serious persuasion from my wife for me to finally agree to it. For most people it would come across as a crazy idea. It's the closest thing to a suicide mission, but either we tried to search for a better life, or we lived in fear and ran the risk of getting needlessly harassed and arrested repeatedly. Those who had well-off family members abroad were able to attain Schengen visas to get to Europe, or some other papers to obtain residence. For a family of three like ours, the chances of obtaining such a visa were slim to none. So, we decided to take the most dangerous route—a route that has claimed thousands of lives over the years.

When you're desperate, you either become too blind to the risks involved or too desperate to care. We decided to go through the Sahara Desert. The agent we found told us that we would be travelling for about six days and that we would arrive in Libya, "insha Allah" which means "God willing". We took his word and prepared enough food and water to last us for a week.

Crossing the Sahara Desert

The journey started at about four o'clock in the morning. After one day, however, one of the cars suddenly broke down and we had to wait five days until the car was fixed. By that point, we were supposed to be in Libya, yet we were still only one day into the journey. Everyone was panicking as the food had almost run out and other resources were low. There was a lot of argument between the travellers and the agent's driver, but the agent said we had to travel together as a group of at least three cars, in case anything happened. We had to wait until the car was fixed. Our group of about thirty-five people was mainly made up of Eritreans, with a couple of Sudanese people with us. The other two cars were transporting Somali people.

Concerns began to grow within our group as to whether we were going to make it or not and what the best way forward was. Some of us felt it was probably best to return to Sudan because it seemed highly unlikely the trip would succeed. The argument was that we had already encountered a setback on the first day which left us stranded for days. There were no guarantees that there wouldn't be any further setbacks. Others insisted that we wait patiently. I was busy with my wife attending to our child and did not involve myself in the argument until someone came to us asking for my opinion. I replied that I would not go back to Sudan, and I'd rather carry on and look forward rather than to look at what I left behind. I said to the group, "Let's pray and sing, for God has the power to bring a solution." As we prayed, I felt empowered and started to write a new song.

> *"You can turn barren wilderness into an oasis."*
> *You can silence the power of storms.*
> *The sun will not harm me during the day.*

"The snare of the enemy will not find me."

I was singing passionately, and the rest of the group clapped their hands and ululated. Everybody felt happy and revived. The next day the agents came with good news. The car was fixed, and we were to continue our journey.

The journey was tough. We were all squashed in the back of a Toyota Hilux. During the day it was extremely hot as we were exposed directly to the sun's rays, but during the night, the temperatures dropped so quickly that it got very cold. It was also the middle of November which made the cold even worse than it normally is.

My wife brought a fluffy blanket for us to share but all the other ladies were not as well prepared, they didn't have any blankets. I decided to give the blanket to the ladies to share with my wife and my daughter. I was sleeping with a group of men without any blankets. The biting cold was so unbearable that I felt it to my core. A night of eight hours felt like eight days.

We tried to make a wall to stop the cold wind, but nothing seemed to work. We even tried to bury our bodies in the sand, but it got worse. I was feeling so cold and miserable that I remember mentally berating myself for being foolish enough to give that blanket away. However, during the day, I used to feel satisfied with my decision to give it up to serve others. It was such a tough journey and tough decisions had to be made throughout.

Oftentimes, the car would get stuck quickly in the sand and we had to use shovels to dig the wheels out. With the sun beating down on our backs, we would have to walk for miles until we found more solid ground, as a heavy load would only end up sinking the car deeper into the sand. At times, we came across human bones and partially buried bodies along our path and everyone would grow silent.

The journey continued for more days—15 more days—and it was very hard. There were two newlywed couples who were supposed to be enjoying their honeymoon on the journey. We would eat together for stronger fellowship and efficiency which helped us to overcome the lack of preparation.

However, some slow eaters like myself struggled on the ride. Being a slow eater meant that the food would disappear before I had my fill. On this one occasion, I had only managed two bites of the food before it was all gone. After such punishment for my slowness, I learned to eat a lot quicker; I think I never stopped eating faster after that experience. A couple of days prior to arriving in Libya we found a small spring and we were able to refill our water jugs. Thank God! We were extremely worried as we nearly ran out of water and food.

After a long and arduous journey, we finally approached the outskirts of Kufra, a Libyan border village. Unfortunately, darkness had already fallen. The driver told us that he had to stop driving for the night because the vehicles' headlights would become too visible for the Libyan soldiers and that would attract unnecessary attention our way. So, he told us to walk. I could see the city in the distance, and I thought the walk would be maybe half an hour. I felt ready and prepared. The ground was sandy, and I could easily feel my feet sinking into the ground. I was holding my daughter in my hands, and I had wrapped her in a big blanket so she wouldn't be exposed to the sand and the cold. We walked for what felt like an eternity.

I felt completely drained after the first hour and the weeks of not eating or drinking had made matters worse. My arms felt extremely weak. But I mustered just about enough energy to carry on. How could I not? The weight of the blanket and my baby in my arms started to weigh heavily on me and it got even heavier with each passing minute. Eventually, my friend Mussie and Efrem came to my rescue and held my daughter for a bit while I rested my arms. After a couple of hours, we made it to Kufra.

Although our journey had taken much longer than we had anticipated we made it without losing anyone. We stayed in Kufra for two days, hiding at a property, while three people Tes, Gabrial and Zewi went out to look for an agent so we could carry on to the capital city, Tripoli. Zewi was a very helpful woman, she was fluent in Arabic, brave and the only child of her parents. She had previously tried to go abroad on several occasions but had not succeeded. Her frustration with how things transpired led her to make the decision to go abroad in search of a better life. She travelled with us through the Sahara Desert. Sitting in the back of the truck had resulted in her developing knee problems. So, the agent made her sit in the passenger cabin with my wife. They really connected on the journey and my wife told me all about her ordeal later.

While they were out searching, a group of Libyan and Sudanese people came to the house with three Land Cruisers to take us. We all jumped in and went on our way. We were under the impression that our team had sent them. After a couple of hours, the Libyan police, who were looking for inmates who had escaped from a nearby prison, apprehended us as we were travelling.

I remember the Libyan soldiers telling us to get out of the vehicles and line up in the field. They searched us thoroughly and took whatever money, gold, and valuable things they could find on us. They asked us what our names were, our religion and where we had come from. Most of our names were foreign to their ears and they struggled to pronounce them. The next question had to do with whether we were Muslims or Christians. Anyone who said 'Christian' ended up getting verbally abused, kicked, and slapped across the face. My prayer of desperation not to be asked that question was miraculously answered as they had stopped before getting to me. Upon interrogation, one of my close friends didn't want to say he was from Eritrea in case they decided to deport us back. Fearing for his life and being nervous, he ended up mentioning three different countries in the process. In the end, they took us all to prison and locked us up.

The Libyan Prison

When we arrived at the prison, we found many migrants from all over Africa who had been there for many months and my heart sank. Everyone was disheartened as we had just survived the challenges of the Sahara. We had been excited to have overcome the desert, only to find ourselves locked behind bars. I will never forget how my wife reacted. She couldn't believe our misfortune after everything that we had been through. She cried a lot. They separated us into different prison halls, the women on one side and the men on the other.

One of the men who travelled with us across the desert approached me. "After everything that we've been through to overcome the hardships of the Sahara, in the end here we are in prison. Where is your God now?" I was very adamant in my reply to him, "This doesn't feel like prison to me; more like a stop for us to rest before we continue with the rest of our journey. All I need to do is stay calm and trust in the Lord." He gave me a very weird look, like I had lost my mind, and he walked away in disbelief. In the prison, we used to sing together and study the Bible to encourage one another and keep up morale. Most of the inmates would listen to us and respect us. One of the songs that I recall was, in fact, in English:

> *"I will sing a new song; I'll glorify His name.*
> *for He is the God of my salvation.*
> *I'll sing a song of adoration.*
> *for He is the God of deliverance.*
> *So let his name be praised in my generation."*

Even though we had only been separated for a brief period. I was missing my wife and my daughter terribly. I couldn't stop thinking about how my wife must have been coping in prison. Sometimes, through the little opening of the prison window, the guards would pass me my daughter so I could see and hold her, and it would lighten the mood in the cell. It taught me that it was always good to focus on positive things, even in the worst situations.

After about four days a government official came to the prison to discuss what was going to happen to us and whether we would be sent back to Eritrea or allowed to stay in the prison. Suddenly he saw my daughter and he was shocked. He commanded that whoever the baby belonged to that her parents be released as soon as possible.

The next morning, we were studying about the personality of Jesus Christ, his name and authority, and his character that makes him different from others. We were then singing songs of praise and worship when I suddenly heard the squeaky sound of the small window opening the door. Then one of the prison guards shouted through the opening in Arabic, "Daniel Habtey minu? Taal hina!" Translated in English, he said, "Who is Daniel Habtey? Come here!" My heart was pounding fast.

Amidst the confusion I approached the guard barefoot. After looking at my state he told me to go put my shoes on and collect my belongings quickly. Deep inside I got the sense that this was good news, but I had to be cautiously optimistic not to get my hopes high only for it to end up being a figment of my imagination.

When I went outside my wife and daughter greeted me. "You're free now! You can go wherever you want." the guard declared. I was so happy but I didn't even get a chance to say goodbye to the friends that I was leaving behind. There were two other pregnant women who were also released with their husbands.

A Sudanese man took us to an abandoned place where we could stay. It had two smaller rooms of good quality and a larger room with dirty floors and no window or door panels. The other two families quickly claimed the two small rooms and we were left with the big room. I was hurt by their selfish actions. The nights were very cold, and draughts would come through the windows. We attempted to board them up but we didn't have the materials to do it properly. Rats and mice would scurry across the floor. The three nights we spent there were so horrible, to the extent that it felt like we had been better off in prison. There was a Libyan man who used to come around and take us to his house to feed us. I will never forget his generosity.

We wanted to go to Tripoli, but I didn't have enough money, and there were no money transfer stations in Kufra. So, while we stayed to figure out our next steps, I would go to see my friends who were still in prison and ask if they needed anything. They had asked me to get them some milk and bread and I would go to the shops and bring it for them. After a couple of days of doing this, my friend Tedros said he had a dream about me. He told me this through the little window.

I could only see his face. He said, "In the dream, we were all sitting in a camp surrounded by the police. Then one of the police officers shouted at you, 'you are free to go! Why are you still here?' You told him you had no money, and the officer told you that you were better off staying then. Then I got up and raised my hands and loudly said, 'I've got the money; I will give it to him.'" Tedros then asked me what his dream meant. I told Tedros that the dream was clear and self-explanatory. He asked me, "Don't you have any money with you?" I said no because we came in a rush from Sudan. He said, "Okay, my brother, I will give you whatever I can." He gave me $400 USD right away. That was a great help, and it was enough to hire an agent and transport to take us to Tripoli. I gave him back the money as soon as I was able to do so.

The agent took us to Tripoli during the night and the trip was uneventful even though my wife remarked that the agent's driving was extremely reckless. She felt he was driving very fast. I sat in the back seat while Senayit sat upfront, pretending to be the driver's wife. She dressed like a local Libyan woman, while I had to hide in the back seat covered with a blanket whenever there was a checkpoint.

After a long night of driving, we arrived in Benghazi. There was an Eritrean man who stayed for years in Libya, and he facilitated permit papers and arranged transport to Tripoli. When we went there, we found many Eritreans, including some of our close friends that we knew in Khartoum. Then we went together on a bus to Tripoli. We were guided to a certain place, which they called 'a chapel', rented by an Eritrean group for Eritrean Christians.

There we found the three people we had mistakenly left behind in Kufra: Tes, Gabriel and Zewi. We hugged each other, told them the story of what happened to us, laughed, and had good fellowship. They asked us why we left without them, and we said that we thought they'd sent the cars and that's why we travelled. We had all seemed perplexed by the chaotic situation, but we were all able to laugh it off after it became evident it had just been a misunderstanding. I am still not sure who sent us those three cars back in Kufra.

Tripoli

Tripoli is a beautiful city, and you can see the influence of Italy in the coffee shops, restaurants, and pastries on display. Many of the buildings looked new and beautiful. Back then, it was the era of Muammar Gaddafi. The people of Libya proudly say that Libya is the best country and cheapest for living expenses. And they were right. The house rent, electricity and particularly food are very cheap. However, some people were not welcoming and were very aggressive, especially towards Eritreans, because they knew that their embassy would not come to their defence if the need arose. After staying there for a few days, we received some money from my friend Kaleb and from my wife's family, especially Kahsay & Alganesh. Their help was timely and highly appreciated because, without it, it would have been very difficult for us to overcome the challenges in Libya.

It was the month of December 2002, so many people were waiting for summer to cross the Mediterranean Sea in good weather. Some of the people we know have already bought a ticket from a popular agent for a safe and reliable ship. I'm not sure why but my heart rushed to leave Libya and to cross the sea as soon as possible. So, I was searching for any available agent and some of my very close friends advised us that it wasn't a good idea to travel at the end of the year. I was told it would be best to wait until the summer months as the waters can be rough and unpredictable in the winter. I hesitated briefly, but again; I had a strong feeling that it was the right time for us to travel. I can't explain it, but I felt the urge to carry on with the journey as planned. It was a bizarre situation where I was feeling hesitant but at the same time, I felt a real calm in my heart. So, I insisted we go ahead with it.

My wife felt it might have been worth heeding the advice we were getting and that perhaps it was best not to rush ahead with our plans. I was adamant this time. I told her, "We're going to do it my way this time. I listened to you in Sudan when we set off for Libya. Now, I need you to listen and trust me." She reluctantly agreed. An Eritrean agent facilitated the trip for us to travel to Zuwara, a coastal city. The agent was so kind to us, he gave us a family discount and he was really looking after us. We arrived in the waiting warehouse where another group of Eritreans were gathered waiting to cross the Mediterranean Sea. Among them was Zewi, the woman who crossed the Sahara Desert with us. My wife was so happy when she saw her there.

After staying there for three days the agent came in the middle of the night, knocked on the door and told us to get up and get ready. We walked from the house to the shore. We were told to be silent, so it was a tense situation. Carrying both a bag and a baby was tiring, and I soon fell to the back of the line.

As I walked slowly with my wife, we bumped into a lady that we knew in Sudan, and she was heavily pregnant. She was happy to see me there because she heard the story of how I assisted my wife when she gave birth to our child. I wondered about how she was going to cope with this journey.

Crossing the Mediterranean Sea

We got to the shore, and they made us sit down and wait for their call. It was still dark and very cold. I embraced my child wrapped in a blanket; thankfully, she was sleeping deeply. The agents were calling one by one, starting with those who were given priority. However, some of them were not patient enough to wait until they were called.

They pushed their way onto the awaiting boat in a desperate bid to get the best seat. And some were understandably anxious, afraid not to be left behind in case the boat got full. We got into a canoe that was going to transport us to the fishing boat. Once we got into the fishing boat we set off. The fishing boat was so low in the water that if I reached down, I could touch the sea.

There were no safety features, no life jackets, and no lights. The sky was covered with dark clouds; it looked like it was ready to rain, and the sea was pitch black. The waves were terrifying. I kept thinking that if anything happened my whole family would disappear. Immediately, I started to regret my decision. In hindsight, I felt it might have been better to wait it out until the summer, but it was too late for a change of heart.

It had already been about a day and a half, and everyone was expecting to arrive in Italy by then. But no one dared ask what was happening. The captain looked busy sailing the boat. He had the face of a North African, probably an Egyptian. Suddenly, he said loudly, "Italia min Allah," and kept saying it a couple of times. It means "Italy is only from God." After a while, he announced that he had lost his sense of direction, had no compass, had no idea where we were, and that the boat had run out of fuel. Panic had set in among the passengers. He looked tired and stressed. In the end, some people got up to help him and they managed to navigate successfully.

Moments later, our eyes caught sight of another vessel—a massive ship—docked in the middle of the sea. The image of the ship is fascinating, resembling a brightly lit city floating in the middle of nowhere.

The sight of this majestic ship reignited a glimmer of hope within each of us, stirring anticipation that this would be our rescue.

The captain urged us to seize this opportune moment by raising our voices as high as possible to catch the attention of the ship's crew. With unwavering determination, he steered our boat closer to the towering ship. The women emerged, their voices echoing across the waters as they cried out for help. Meanwhile, the men frantically waved their arms, and some even resorted to setting garments ablaze to enhance our visibility.

As we drew nearer to the ship, instead of extending a helping hand, they deployed water jets to repel us. Only then did our captain grasp the unfolding situation, understanding the imminent peril we faced. Swiftly, he veered our boat away from the ship, much to the dismay of us all. Frustration enveloped the group, with some venting their grievances and directing curses towards the ship's crew for their apparent indifference.

Yet, in the midst of our desperation, the motive behind the ship's actions eluded us. It wasn't until later reflection that we conjectured they may have been apprehensive of our approaching vessel, perhaps fearing us to be bandits or pirates.

Though our hopes were shattered in that moment, the realisation dawned upon us with hindsight. As we continued to sail, all the women returned to their designated places below deck where the engines were located. My wife and the pregnant women remained hidden below deck and did not come out to express their concern, prompting me to check on my family. As my wife asked me, "What is going on?", I reassured her by saying, "its fine, darling." Are we there yet?

"I said, 'We are nearly there, just keep praying,' then I asked her how our baby was doing to change the subject and distract her. My wife replied that our baby had been sleeping the whole time. I remarked that it was a true blessing that the baby wasn't causing her any trouble during the journey, to which my wife agreed."

While I was on the engine deck talking to my wife and a pregnant woman, the captain spotted another large vessel that looked similar to the one we had seen before. Deciding it was our best chance for help, the captain made the decision to chase after the ship in hopes of receiving supplies like food, fuel, or safety features such as life jackets. He instructed the passengers to sit properly as he tried to speed up our boat.

Despite our boat's speed and the powerful crashing waves pushing us forward, we ended up colliding with the other ship. A loud bumping sound made me rush out of the engine deck to see what had happened. The captain was visibly upset and frustrated, stating that he didn't understand why we were being denied help and that the situation was crazy. Water began flooding into the boat through a hole on the right side, causing panic among the passengers.

Amid the chaos, some individuals, like a man named Haile, began scooping the water out with a makeshift bucket and rope. I joined in to help, but as we grew tired, we called upon the other passengers for assistance. However, their lack of interest and willingness to help frustrated us greatly. Haile tried to convince them to pitch in, but some reacted with indifference, stating they didn't care.

Tensions escalated as the situation seemed dire. Everyone was on edge, unsure of what would happen next. It was a moment of despair and desperation as we struggled to keep the boat afloat.

The Peace Child

To make matters worse, the mother, who was expecting a baby, went into active labour. She kept calling my name, pleading for help, knowing I had some medical experience.

I rushed to the deck below and found her in agonising pain, exacerbated by our dire situation, stranded in the middle of nowhere. I lacked the basic tools needed for a safe delivery: no light, no gloves, and no medical equipment. When faced with such circumstances, one can't help but wonder if miracles are possible even in the direst situations, or if they only add chaos to the already overwhelming turmoil. Yet, this birth was a sign that amidst the darkness, there can be a glimmer of light. Despite the damaged torch and the pitch darkness, I carefully examined the situation, feeling for signs of progress in the labour. As I felt the baby's head, I realised the urgency of the situation and swiftly communicated with the mother amidst the roar of the boat's engine, urging her not to push until I gave the signal.

In the dimly lit confines of the small boat, the mother's cries of anguish echoed with each wave that rocked us, signalling the imminent arrival of new life. As her labour intensified, her distress became palpable amidst the chaos of our uncertain journey. Urgency hung in the air as I urged her to summon her last reserves of strength, her determination clear in the lines of her face. In a final, desperate push, a tiny bundle emerged, welcomed into the world with a chorus of relief and gratitude. The newborn's cries confirmed its arrival.

I cleared my throat and instructed the woman not to push any further, hoping she could hear me over the loud engine noise. I searched through my bag for a razor blade to cut the umbilical cord, but my heart sank as I realised I lacked medical forceps, clamps, string, or rope. The urgency grew with each lurch of the boat. I called out to the six women inside the deck for help, but they remained frozen in shock, unresponsive to my pleas. Frustration overtook me as I yelled, "Can't you see I need a hand over here?"

Finally, turning to Haile, who I knew was the most helpful and reliable person on-board, I asked if he had anything that could help. Sadly, he also didn't have any medical supplies but offered his shoelace. Despite my surprise at his choice of footwear for the journey, his smart leather shoelace proved to be just what we needed to successfully complete the task at hand. Though it may not have been the ideal situation, we made the best of what we had and were able to successfully complete the necessary job.

With trembling hands, I swiftly wrapped the newborn in towels from my wife's bag, creating a makeshift cocoon to protect it from our harsh surroundings. Expecting jubilation, I was met with subdued reactions from the passengers, their expressions clouded with apprehension. I attempted to infuse a sense of celebration, exclaiming praises and words of gratitude, but my efforts seemed futile. Their despair stemmed from the overwhelming circumstances and the belief in the futility of new life. Despite the commotion, the birth of the "peace child" brought a sense that the worst was behind us. Amidst the chaos and uncertainty of the Mediterranean Sea, in the heart of a turbulent journey aboard a small boat lacking safety features, a miracle unfolded. A baby boy came into the world, his first cries piercing through the tension and fear that gripped the vessel. It was a moment of both immense joy and profound concern, as the fragile newborn entered a world fraught with peril and uncertainty. Yet, during adversity, his birth brought a glimmer of hope and renewed determination to persevere against the odds. Miraculously, the waves calmed, and the boat picked up speed. Hours later, we saw a distant mountain, sparking early celebrations. As pessimism crept back, someone shouted, "I see birds!" signalling we were close to shore. Excitement and hope revived within us.

The oldest passenger, Medhanie, nicknamed "Kabila," encouraged us to cheer for the captain. The collective cheer uplifted spirits, and we started feeling more settled.

The atmosphere among the passengers lightened, and conversations began to flow more freely. Shortly after the chaotic birth on board, a concerned individual approached me, inquiring about the whereabouts of the mother's trousers. I explained that I had disposed of them in the sea due to the heavy bloodstains. To my dismay, his countenance darkened as he revealed the unfortunate truth hidden within one of the pockets was approximately a thousand dollars. The man had entrusted the money to the mother, confident that her condition would deter any searches. Unfortunately, this vital information had not been relayed to me, resulting in a significant loss. Despite the disappointment, the arrival of the precious baby boy served as a beacon of hope in our tumultuous journey.

After enduring more than 48 hours at sea, we finally reached the shores of Lampedusa, the southernmost island of Italy. The marine police greeted us, and the significance of the island's name, "Lampedusa," meaning "bright light after darkness," resonated deeply with our experiences. Typically, the journey from Zuwara to Lampedusa spans 12-14 hours, but our ordeal had stretched far beyond that timeframe.

The police officers came aboard and started to take us onshore one by one. Haile, the most helpful person in the group, spoke Italian fluently and informed the police about the newborn baby. The officers exclaimed, "Mamma mia, c'è un bambino, there is a new-born baby!" They immediately took the mother and her baby to the hospital.

The rest of us were taken to a camp that resembled a detention centre. It was hard to believe, yet I felt an overwhelming sense of relief, leaving me at a loss for words. What a relief! I could only utter expressions of gratitude: "Thank you, God, for your mercy and divine protection throughout this journey." Everyone else seemed equally elated. One of my close friends, Bereket, expressed his joy by performing a celebratory headstand! I joined in his jubilation, but exhaustion soon overtook us, and we fell into a deep sleep until the next morning.

When we woke up, we discovered that our belongings, and some money had been taken. Some North African immigrants had taken advantage of our fatigue and helped themselves to our belongings while we slept. After discussing amongst ourselves, one of the ladies who witnessed the theft mentioned seeing them pilfering our possessions. Politely, we approached them, asking for the return of our stolen items, but our appeals fell on deaf ears. The group of Eritreans had been prepared for any possible conflicts, and the situation quickly escalated into a physical confrontation, with punches and kicks exchanged. It required intervention from the police guards to de-escalate the situation, eventually resulting in the recovery of most of our belongings. While Eritreans are not typically known for instigating trouble, they are also not ones to overlook attempts to take what rightfully belongs to them.

The following day was like a rollercoaster of nerves for me. I was summoned by the police and taken to the immigration office. To be honest, with the language barrier, my mind was racing with uncertainty and fear. As I walked into the imposing building, my heart pounded in my chest, and my palms grew clammy with nervousness. The unknown loomed over me, casting a shadow of unease.

But as I entered the immigration office, a wave of relief washed over me, only to be replaced by a different kind of apprehension. They invited me for a special cake and cappuccino, creating a pleasant atmosphere. There, I found myself face to face with a professional medical nurse and a friendly immigration officer. They spoke fluent English and were eager to hear about the unique experience of delivering the baby on the boat. They even shared a similar case from 30 years ago, adding a touch of familiarity to the conversation.

With their warm approach, the questions about my medical background and the extraordinary event that brought me to them felt less intimidating. As they delved into my experience in the medical field, the delivery of the baby, and the sequence of events that transpired, I felt the weight of the situation pressing down on me. Nevertheless, I summoned the courage to recount every detail, right down to the moment when a simple shoelace became a lifeline in tying the umbilical cord.

To my surprise, the tension in the room dissipated when they chuckled at the absurdity and ingenuity of my impromptu solution. Their initial amusement quickly turned to admiration for the resourcefulness I displayed in a moment of crisis, filling me with a sense of pride that overshadowed the earlier fear.

Ultimately, what started as a nerve-wracking ordeal turned into an unexpected opportunity to showcase my resilience and quick thinking. As I left the immigration office that day, I couldn't help but feel a sense of accomplishment, knowing that despite the challenges, I had faced them head-on and emerged stronger for it. After inquiring about the well being of the mother and baby, they reassured me that both were in good health. The nurse extended her congratulations, stating, "You were the right person, in the right place, at the right time—it was truly a miracle. It was by God's grace that you were on that boat. Just imagine what could have happened if you had not been there! The mother could have faced serious challenges during the delivery." Their words of encouragement lifted my spirits as I was allowed to return to the camp, relieved to hear that the mother and her baby boy were doing well.

Christmas Celebration in Crotone

After three days, we once again found ourselves boarding a boat to cross the sea and reach the mainland, with our final destination being Crotone in the Calabria province. Although we had hoped to travel by plane, fate had other plans and we were back on a boat. Many of us were looking forward to our first flight, but it was not meant to be. The boat ride brought back memories of our difficult crossing of the Mediterranean Sea, but this time the vessel was sturdy, well-equipped with safety features, and well-lit, making the experience much more pleasant overall.

Calabria, the southernmost region in Italy, is known for its stunning beauty. After a short break on the mainland, we were instructed to continue our journey to Crotone by bus. The trip ended up being longer than expected, but we were completely taken aback by the lush landscapes, picturesque bridges, and vibrant green fields we passed along the way. The mountains in the distance added to the beauty of the scene, while well-tended gardens filled with colourful flowers added a touch of charm.

Despite feeling a bit drowsy after the long journey, I couldn't help but appreciate the beauty of Calabria. My wife, on the other hand, was completely captivated by the scenery and felt a deep connection to the land. She reminisced about her own mother and how she used to speak of the beauty of Italy, which only added to her appreciation for the province. Calabria truly is a breath-taking place.

After nearly a full day of travel, we finally arrived at a large refugee camp. A palpable sense of relief and joy filled the air as our long-held dreams had finally come to fruition after a gruelling and tumultuous journey. We stayed in the camp for a month, during which time all the passengers shared their experiences, laughed, and dined together. I recall singing every night and sharing the word of God with them. We shared moments of fun and joy together.

As Christmas drew near, we eagerly looked forward to celebrating the festive season in this unfamiliar territory. Little did we know that our arrival in Italy, after enduring the treacherous journey across the Mediterranean, would feel like entering a whole new world. Stepping onto Italian soil, we were met with a lively and welcoming atmosphere, enveloped in the spirit of Christmas.

Despite the hardships we faced at sea, a sense of hope and renewal filled the air as we embraced the joy and fresh beginnings the season brought. The streets were alive with twinkling lights and vibrant decorations, evoking a sense of wonder and gratitude within us for our safe arrival.

The birth of a baby boy during our voyage added an extra touch of magic to our holiday celebrations, reminding us of the beauty and miracle of life. As we shared our journey with the Italian locals, we were met with kindness and hospitality, warmly embraced by their community, and making us feel at home in this new land.

The Italians were incredibly friendly, allowing us to partake in traditional Italian Christmas customs. We savoured the rich flavours of festive cuisine and joined in joyful carols sung in the streets. The laughter of children reverberated through the cobblestone alleys, blending with the melodious sound of church bells ringing out across the town.

During such jubilation, we marvelled at the miracle of life and the resilience of the human spirit. Despite the trials we had endured, the birth of a new baby boy filled us with hope for the future and a renewed sense of purpose. As we exchanged embraces and well wishes with those around us, we felt deeply grateful for the gift of life and the opportunity to start anew in this beautiful land.

Indeed, celebrating Christmas in Italy after our perilous journey was a testament to the power of hope, faith, and community. With each joyful moment shared with the Italian people, we felt a sense of belonging and gratitude for the blessings bestowed upon us. And as we welcomed the dawn of a new year, we embraced the promise of brighter days ahead, united by the bonds of love and the spirit of Christmas.

On Christmas Eve, the residents of Crotone were excited to learn about the arrival of a new baby on our journey. The local newspaper featured a photo of the mother and her baby on one page, with Mary and Jesus on the other side. The newspaper also shared a similar story from 30 years ago, when an Italian woman gave birth on the same island. This news spread quickly, and the people of Crotone joyfully joined us in celebrating the special occasion. A variety of food, cakes, chocolates, and drinks were prepared for everyone at the camp to enjoy.

The Italian priest arrived and shared a Christmas story with us. Although the language barrier prevented clear understanding, it was a joy to celebrate with the local community. The priest concluded with a prayer, met with a chorus of "Amen" from everyone present. However, the mood shifted abruptly as a few migrants rushed towards the feast table, greedily grabbing food, cake, and chocolate. Their actions were shocking and disgraceful, causing chaos and distress for all witnesses. The priest and locals were left in disbelief, ultimately deciding to leave the scene. They had come to join in the festivities but were appalled by the unacceptable behaviour displayed by a small number of individuals.

The incident left a bitter taste in everyone's mouth, including myself, as I had hoped to surprise my wife with a piece of cake but left empty-handed. The refugees, who had previously shown devotion through prayer and worship, demonstrated a complete lack of discipline and decorum on what was meant to be a special evening. Their actions, characterised by impatience and a lack of civility, tarnished what should have been a joyous occasion for all involved. The priest and the locals left in dismay, having come to celebrate and share their love, only to be met with such disrespectful behaviour.

I had intended to surprise my wife with some cake, but I left the event empty-handed. Their careless behaviour made me feel embarrassed and frustrated. The migrants had arrived at the camp before us and had a routine of praying and singing worship songs every morning. I had previously admired their dedication to prayer and worship. However, their behaviour in the presence of the priest and local community during what should have been a memorable celebration was disgraceful.

We stayed there for about a month, and we were able to make phone calls to Libya to learn about the fate of the group that had crossed the Sahara Desert with us. They had been told they would be deported back to Eritrea, but they were still being kept in prison. We began to pray on their behalf so that they would not be deported to Eritrea. Unfortunately, there had been more bad news. Zewi, the woman who was close with my wife during the journey, went missing after she set off from Libya to Italy with hundreds of people. We tried to locate her, but her whereabouts remain unknown to this day.

There were rumours that during the same week we set off from Zuwara there were at least three boats packed with hundreds of migrants who had gone missing. It might just be the case that Zewi could have been among those that went missing. The way this generation ended up fleeing their homeland and dying in the Mediterranean Sea is beyond tragic. These were people who had a home and a bright future, but they were forced to leave it all behind because of bad governance.

After staying for a month, we were released from the camp in Crotone. They told us we were free to go wherever we wanted. So we went to Rome, the ancient city of the former colony of Eritrea. Rome is a beautiful city that reminded me of Asmara. The architecture of the buildings, the coffee shops and the restaurants really took me back to my own home city. Some Eritreans led us to make use of an abandoned building.

There had already been a lot of Eritreans staying there. The building was so crowded and dilapidated that my wife was shocked. My daughter couldn't stop crying. It was difficult for us to stay there. We had decided to spend a couple of days in a hotel, but soon our money was about to run out. So, we looked for a charity house to stay at temporarily.

Finally, we managed to find a place in charity housing, which was a great help at that time. The Eritrean Full Gospel Church in Rome was so encouraging, their welcome was unforgettable.

A friend from my time in Sawa and Sudan, Bahre, organised an event where I was invited to minister at an Eritrean church in Florence. Although the church congregation was small, we had a memorable time together. Despite the warmth and family-oriented nature of Italians, it was challenging to secure employment and housing without proper documentation. The Eritrean fellowship in Florence provided a sense of community and respect that I will always treasure. Despite the language barrier, the policy and limited job opportunities in Italy, the Italian people are truly welcoming, friend- and family-oriented. Ultimately, my family and I made the decision to relocate to the UK.

The UK is heralded as a land of freedom, where democracy, law, and dignity prevail. This contrast to the oppressive dictatorship in my home country is what compelled me to leave in search of a better life. The journey and challenges faced along the way have been worth it, as the UK has provided me with a sense of dignity and respect that I never experienced before.

In the UK, I have found an environment where freedom of expression is protected, where the rule of law is upheld, and where democracy thrives. This has allowed me to work, practise my faith without fear, voice my political opinions, and engage in the democratic process by voting for the party that aligns with my values. These rights and freedoms are not taken for granted, as they represent an incredible blessing that was not available to me in my home country.

The UK's commitment to freedom, law, democracy, and dignity has made it an ideal destination for refugees, especially Eritreans like me. It has become our promised land, a place where we can build a better future and be treated with the respect and humanity that every individual deserves. The opportunity to live in a country that cherishes these values is truly invaluable, and I am grateful for the refuge and opportunity that the UK has provided to me and my family.

The situation in Eritrea has remained dire and unchanged for the past 32 years under the same oppressive regime, with a single party in power and no democratic elections held. The regime's crackdown on dissent and persecution of those with differing political views or beliefs has led to countless human rights violations and tragic consequences.

Individuals who have been imprisoned for their faith or political views have endured years of suffering, with some languishing in Eritrean prisons for two decades or more. The lack of due process and basic human rights in these prisons is a grave concern, as these individuals are held captive without any hope of release or justice.

Many Eritreans have been forced to flee their homeland in search of safety and a better future, facing perilous journeys through the Sahara Desert and across the Mediterranean Sea. Tragically, some never make it to their intended destinations, losing their lives along the way. Those who do survive often face difficult and uncertain circumstances in refugee camps or conscience prisoners.

The plight of those who have been unjustly imprisoned, lost their lives during migration, or continue to endure hardships is a heartbreaking reality that weighs heavily on the hearts of many. The lack of change and progress in Eritrea over the past three decades is a stark reminder of the on-going human rights abuses and challenges faced by its people. The hope for a brighter future and for justice to prevail remains a distant dream for many, leaving a deep sense of sorrow and concern for the future of Eritrea.

Upon my arrival in the UK, I embarked on the recording of my third album. In a moment of reflection, I felt compelled to use this opportunity to support the families of individuals who have been unjustly detained. My aim was to not only raise awareness on their plight but also to offer a semblance of hope to those enduring the anguish of separation.

I dedicated this album to all those who are patiently awaiting the day of their loved ones' release. In an effort to provide tangible support, a portion of the proceeds from the album were directed towards the families of the imprisoned individuals, who have suffered for daring to express their beliefs or political viewpoints.

While I recognize that there is always more that can be done in such circumstances, I humbly acknowledge that my contributions may seem insignificant in the grand scheme of things. Nevertheless, it was my way of demonstrating to these individuals that they have not been forgotten, that their struggles have not gone unnoticed. Through this small gesture, I hoped to provide some solace and solidarity to those facing such immense challenges.

This journey has undeniably been one of the most challenging experiences in my life. However, it has taught me a vital lesson: the development of a constructive character is of utmost importance. Throughout different phases of my life, I have faced failures and obstacles that put my core values to the test. It is during these difficult times that the true essence of one's character shines through.

Reflecting on the journey from Eritrea to the UK, I cannot overlook the arduous and challenging path I traversed, navigating through unfamiliar territories, diverse cultures, varying policies, and languages. In such circumstances, taking calculated risks became essential to find a way out of the entrapment and move towards a brighter future.

Courage proved to be a guiding force in times of crisis and uncertainty. It enabled me to overcome obstacles and forge ahead despite the challenges that confronted me along the way. However, amidst the trials and tribulations, it was the embodiment of good character that emerged as the most invaluable asset.

Regardless of the circumstances or external influences, maintaining a strong moral character stands as a beacon of integrity and resilience. While external circumstances may fluctuate and material possessions may diminish in significance, the enduring impact of one's character remains ever-present.

The acts of kindness, generosity, and solidarity that I encountered in Sudan left an indelible mark on my soul. The spirit of sharing, caring, and selflessness displayed during moments of scarcity and adversity exemplified the true essence of humanity.

These profound experiences serve as a poignant reminder of the enduring power of human character. They inspire me to cultivate and exemplify these virtues in my own life, striving to extend kindness, compassion, and support to others. In doing so, I aim to create a legacy of benevolence and empathy that transcends temporal boundaries and resonates with the essence of humanity.

QUESTIONS AND SELF-REFLECTION FOR PRACTICAL STEPS

Question 1

What lessons have you learned from this chapter?

Question 2

Who are you? What are your beliefs and values?

Question 3

How have your experiences in life shaped your character?

Question 4

How willing are you to accept criticism? What is your attitude toward criticism?

Question 5

Are you intentional about developing your character as you journey through life?

Chapter 6

LEARNING AND AIMING FOR EXCELLENCE

When we applied for asylum, the British Home Office placed us in Newcastle upon Tyne. It was a stroke of luck that we were able to reconnect with our closest friends - my wife with Saron and myself with Sirak. We found ourselves settling into the city quite comfortably. Even though I had more opportunities among the Eritrean community in England at that time, we made a conscious decision to make Newcastle upon Tyne our home.

For three years, life in Newcastle upon Tyne was swift and enjoyable. The good news from the Home Office arrived quickly, bringing great relief to my wife and me, as we were anxious. The atmosphere was tense, as my interview occurred just days after the London bombings on July 7th. We anxiously checked the mail every day. When the good news finally arrived within a month, I read it multiple times in disbelief. To ensure I wasn't dreaming, I phoned my friend Sirak, who confirmed it. We were overjoyed, celebrated, and thanked God. My wife cooked a delicious Habesha meal, and Sirak, who loved injera, along with other friends, joined us.

Afterward, I became very enthusiastic. The Eritrean church was ready for growth, both in number and spiritual understanding. I was involved in interpreting, giving my testimony in courts, and community services, all of which helped the church grow rapidly.

God blessed us with a third child, our son Adoniram, born in Newcastle upon Tyne. He was a healthy and adorable boy, bringing us much joy and gratitude. Unlike the anxiety that accompanied the birth of my first child, Adoniram's arrival was a smoother experience.

However, one particular moment stands out as one of the most challenging parenting experiences I have faced to date. It was a Monday morning, and after a night of restless sleep, I found myself feeling drowsy. My wife had plans to return home shortly after dropping off our daughters at school, entrusting me with the task of looking after Adoniram until she could take him to school in the afternoon. As I awaited her return, I unintentionally drifted off to sleep on the sofa, with my son playing in the living room.

When I awoke and couldn't locate my son in the room, panic immediately set in. Frantically calling out his name yielded no response, and my search under the sofa turned up empty. Ruled out from being able to open the door himself due to his young age and the handle's height, I scoured every possible hiding spot, including the closet, to no avail.

Increasingly frantic, I resorted to shouting his name at the top of my lungs, desperately hoping for a sign of his whereabouts. The realisation that he was nowhere to be found sent me into a state of sheer terror. Attempts to reach my wife failed, and it dawned on me that she had left her phone behind. With nerves on edge, I resolved to canvass the neighbourhood in search of my missing son, braving the pouring rain in nothing but my pyjamas.

Despite thorough efforts that led me to the school entrance, my search proved futile. Overwhelmed by a sense of helplessness and dread, I made the difficult decision to return home and seek assistance from the authorities. Swiftly responding to the call for help, they combed through the house with the same urgency and thoroughness that I had earlier displayed.

As the authorities continued their search for my missing son, my wife unexpectedly arrived home. Feeling the weight of the situation bearing down on me, I braced myself for the daunting task of breaking the news to her. However, before I could utter a word, she questioned the presence of the police with a perplexed expression.

With a heavy heart, I confessed to her that I had been unable to locate Adoniram despite an exhaustive search. It was then that she revealed the truth - our son was not lost, but rather safely at school attending the playgroup. A wave of relief washed over me, washing away the fear and anxiety that had consumed me. Without hesitation, I relayed the good news to the authorities, signalling an end to their search.

Despite the initial panic and overwhelming emotions, the joy of knowing that our son was safe, and sound overshadowed the moment of distress and miscommunication. The sense of relief and gratitude filled the air, turning what had seemed like a nightmare into a moment of sheer bliss.

Living in Newcastle upon Tyne offered me a chance to immerse myself in the city's beauty and vibrancy. The Tyne River, winding its way between Newcastle and Gateshead, provided a breath-taking backdrop for my everyday life. I have fond memories of watching as people jogged along the riverbanks, soaking up the summer sun and enjoying the serene atmosphere. The cafes and pubs that lined the Quayside added to the charm of the area, bustling with activity, and creating a welcoming environment for residents and visitors alike.

My friend Sirak introduced us to a wonderful family. We are forever grateful for the kindness and friendship shown to us by Ron and Jenda Harbottle. Their warm hearts and genuine interest in our family's well-being during our integration journey will always be remembered. Their willingness to embrace our culture and traditions, such as enjoying Eritrean cuisine and participating in the traditional coffee ceremony, truly touched our hearts. Our children still speak fondly of the special moments shared with them in Hexham. The Harbottles are truly remarkable individuals, and we are blessed to have crossed paths with them.

They helped us invite my mother-in-law Zehaytu to visit us, and through their assistance, the UK embassy provided her with a visa to stay with us. This brought immense joy to my wife and children. My kids were truly blessed to meet their grandmother in person. My mother-in-law stayed with us for nearly nine months, and we cherished every moment with her. She is a beautiful person, both inside and out. Her radiant smile and humble nature are truly remarkable. Her cooking is incredibly delicious, but most impressive of all is her wonderful character. She never complained, gossiped, or engaged in any meaningless talk. Additionally, she was always eager to hear the word of God. Every night, we would enjoy a coffee ceremony while reading the Bible together. I will never forget what she once said: "I have never been this happy in my life." Senayit, her youngest daughter, was overjoyed to see her mother spend time with her grandchildren from a loving family. Sadly, my mother-in-law passed away after returning home to Eritrea. We will always remember her beautiful character and delicious food with fondness.

Additionally, I had the opportunity to connect with Pastor Ken and Lois Gott, senior pastors of Bethshan church, who had previously led churches in Newcastle and Sunderland. As the Eritrean church continued to grow, we faced resource constraints in our youth ministry. So,

I began discussing the possibility of affiliating with their church for the benefit of our second generation. Ken and Lois were enthusiastic and welcomed me even more than I had anticipated. They were eager to offer their assistance and mentorship. Regrettably, one of the Eritrean church leaders disagreed with the idea of affiliation with a British church. I felt obliged to decide against the move to maintain unity within the church and avoid a church split.

Overall, my time in Newcastle was not only a period of personal and spiritual growth but also a rewarding opportunity to contribute to the welfare and integration of those in need within the Eritrean community and beyond.

One memory that stands out is the pleasure of strolling along the river with my dear friends J Bereke, and Tes. The camaraderie and fellowship during coffee ceremonies with my wife's friends Martha, Elilta, and Saron will forever hold a special place in my heart. These moments serve as a testament to the strong bonds we shared.

However, after three sweet years, I stepped down from my pastoral duties. It was one of the most difficult decisions of my life—not the stepping down itself, but the weight of the responsibility. It's hard to explain, but I knew stepping down wouldn't solve all problems, yet it was the best option for me.

My greatest concern was preventing a potential split in the church. I was determined not to let that happen under my watch, but it was not an easy decision. Regardless, I often felt like the scapegoat for every problem.

For two years, I felt lonely, confused, and heartbroken. I was separated from the church, and it felt like people only cared when I held a church position. Without it, it seemed no one cared. The only solace I found during that time was a small circle of friends, especially my faithful friend Tes. We often walked by the Tyne River on the quayside, drank coffee at side cafes, and remained in touch.

During that time, I was unsure what my next steps should be. I spent two years studying, waiting, and preparing for any opportunity. To be honest, I found it hard to discern exactly what to do. My soul was troubled not because I couldn't find something to do, but because I didn't want to waste my time on something that wouldn't last. I wanted to pursue something I was passionate about and sincerely sought to follow God's will for my life.

I tried to start a business in partnership with an Eritrean friend. I sent him a considerable amount of money to buy some items from Dubai. Unfortunately, my friend was arrested in Asmara and remains in prison to this day. It was a significant financial loss, but more importantly, I was deeply concerned about his situation. He was intelligent, multi-talented, and a business owner. However, his case has never been brought to court, and justice has eluded him for 16 years.

I was very frustrated. Most of my time was spent searching and studying to recover from the loss. I was so dedicated that at times, I spent more than 16 hours a day working. I remember my eyesight deteriorating and struggling with insomnia. Despite my efforts, I found no success. Then, my wife encouraged me to pursue my old career as a health assistant and upgrade it to become a medical doctor. Another Eritrean friend from the USA pointed out that nurses and health assistants could earn a significant amount of money in the USA and urged me to consider moving. Despite these options, my soul remained restless. I struggled to choose the right path, knowing that God had called me for a specific purpose since 1996 and that I had been very productive back home in Eritrea.

Finally, an American friend invited me to a conference in Nottingham. There, God spoke to me through a young woman who was sharing her life testimony. Despite achieving her dream job, great income, and a house, God spoke to her about becoming a missionary in another country. She accepted God's calling gladly and now leads a joyful life, even with less money.

From this experience, I learned that achieving your dreams is wonderful. However, achieving God's dream for your life and living according to His will is the ultimate joy, the most fulfilling and rewarding path.

After the conference, I prayed and sought God's will for my life. I realized the importance of following God's plan, immersing myself in society, learning about different cultures, and striving for excellence. This journey was focused on gaining a deeper understanding of important issues such as persecution, immigration, integration, and opportunities for future generations.

As I prepared to take practical steps forward, I acknowledged that a return to my home country was not in the near future, despite my strong desire to do so. I began searching for opportunities that would facilitate this transition, but I was unsure of how and when it would happen. Therefore, I patiently waited for a better opportunity to arise.

During a visit to my friend, Habtom, a pastor in Sheffield, I had the unexpected encounter with another Eritrean acquaintance, Kahsay, who resided in Huddersfield. Kahsay extended an invitation for me to preach at their Eritrean fellowship and introduced me to Pastor Hannam, the senior pastor at the Elim Pentecostal Church in Huddersfield at that time.

Engaging in an extensive conversation with Pastor Hannam, we delved into my background, experiences, and my vision for facilitating the integration of refugees and fostering a brighter future for the second generation. He mentioned that the church had been actively seeking an individual with a diverse cultural background and genuine experience in engaging with individuals from various cultures. Their quest had spanned several years, aligning providentially with my patient wait and prayers for a potential opportunity. This revelation filled me with a sense of fulfilment, as if I had finally stumbled upon what I had been earnestly seeking: a remarkable chance to interact with individuals from diverse backgrounds while also contributing to the advancement of my own community. My heartfelt aspiration was to immerse myself in a new culture, bolster my qualifications, and discover a platform for the actualization of my vision.

In 2010, my family and I relocated from Newcastle upon Tyne to Huddersfield, West Yorkshire, where the Elim church welcomed me warmly. Although my family was initially hesitant about leaving Newcastle, particularly my wife, who was reluctant to part with her friends and the comfort of familiar surroundings, the love and care extended by the Elim church eventually provided solace for her. For me personally, the guidance and support I received from Peter and Kath Hannam proved to be invaluable for my ministry and ministerial studies.

Assuming my position as a part-time church worker, my primary responsibility revolved around overseeing and ministering to the Eritrean community. Our primary objective was to facilitate the integration of both myself and the Eritrean fellowship into the church community. Despite my previous experience and qualifications, I was enthusiastic to start afresh within the denomination to achieve this goal.

This experience proved to be enriching for me, offering ample opportunities for learning, and building connections with others. Concurrently, I pursued leadership qualifications with the aspiration of becoming a Minister in Training (MIT). Embracing the process of ordination, I engaged in rigorous training sessions encompassing preaching techniques, active participation in elders' meetings, and collaborative work within a small subcommittee. Though some aspects of the process overlapped with my previous qualifications from the School of Leadership Training (SLT) back home, I derived immense benefit from the experience. It inspired me to pursue further education, organise integration training, and conduct research for potential doctoral degrees focusing on integration.

I have had the privilege of being enriched by both the Eritrean fellowship and Elim church here in Huddersfield. The leaders at Elim, particularly Senior Pastor Mike Read, are incredibly kind, relational, and embody the spirit of servant leadership.

I was also trying to bridge the gap and to facilitate integration for the benefit of the whole community. The most important skill that I've learned from the Elim leadership is the ability to work together as a team. The civility, respect, and heart to be gracious to one another that I have witnessed has been incredible. The ability to express minds and choose their words carefully and wisely is fascinating. Their punctuality and time management efficiency are highly appreciated. However, I realised that every culture has its own strength and weakness. In this case, there was a time where I perceived a lack of passion and intentionality in our church, and I was not always sure how to continue with my contribution on integration.

On the other hand, the Eritrean fellowship has an incredible passion and enthusiasm for prayer and worship. Their hospitality and fellowship are amazing. In general, Eritreans are very genuine people; however, this can also mean that when we get angry or disagree with something, the whole community ends up knowing about it because our emotions get the better of us and we end up expressing ourselves publicly. We are not always good at teamwork as typically Eritreans are quite headstrong and single minded. Things can very quickly reach disagreements as we don't express our minds wisely. To assist integration properly both cultures need to learn from each other. Imagine if both groups were determined to complement each other, it would be the best community.

During my tenure in Huddersfield, I encountered certain challenges, particularly in the realm of communication when faced with regional slang and accents, especially during fast-paced conversations. Upon returning home, I often sought clarification from my children regarding unfamiliar phrases. Consequently, I was eager to boldly practise facilitating quicker integration while remaining cautious and mindful not to inadvertently embarrass my children in social settings.

I have a vivid memory of my first invitation to deliver a sermon in English at Elim Church. Despite my nervousness, the feedback I received was surprisingly positive and insightful. One gentleman's comment humbled me: "Your passion is admirable, but it seemed to overshadow the message in your sermon." This struck a chord with me. While passion is a characteristic often associated with African people, I realised the significance of balancing passion with substantial content to truly convey the message effectively.

For example, Eritreans are known for their tradition of prayer and passionate singing, which can be uplifting and spiritually enriching. On the other hand, Elim Huddersfield appears to be very structured, strategic, and focused on critical thinking. This contrast in styles has piqued my interest and further motivated me to delve deeper into my research.

However, my fundamental goal remains to provide support to the community that embraced me warmly, as well as to displaced nationals, refugees, and the generations that follow, assisting them in their journey to seamlessly integrate into the broader church community. With each step forward, I am confident that significant strides have been made in realising these objectives.

Integration

I always say I love Britain except for the weather. British weather is so different from Eritrea. When we first arrived in Newcastle upon Tyne during the summer, people were talking about the weather and the sunshine, which I didn't fully understand at the time. However, a couple of months later, the leaves began to fall, and the winter was cold, with typical snow and heavy rain. Coming from a country with thirteen months of sunshine, always sunny and beautiful, it was quite a change. So, when it is sunny, I make sure to make the most of it.

However, my wife appreciated the four different seasons, instead of having just one season all year round. She makes the most of each season, such as creating a cosy atmosphere during winter by burning firewood and drinking hot chocolate and enjoying barbecues and picnics during the summertime.

However, integration and achieving God's will is more important than external weather. So far my few experiences have led me to realise that no matter how long one has been here or how proficiently one speaks the language, there are still potential cultural differences to uncover every day. I believe these differences are worthwhile to research and document to enhance the process of integration, reconcile differences, and educate community and church leaders.

Living in the UK has been a profoundly enriching experience for me. In many ways, I consider myself among the most fortunate individuals in the world to have the opportunity to call this place home. It's fascinating to reflect on how, despite it not being my initial dream to come here, I have developed a deep love and appreciation for this country. The only drawback is the weather — a topic that seems to unite many who reside here! The unpredictable nature of British weather often poses a challenge, but it pales in comparison to what I left behind.

One of the key aspects I've learned about life in the UK is the significance of integration. It's not just about residing in this country; it's about immersing oneself in its culture, traditions, and way of life. By embracing the values and customs of the UK, one can truly make the most of what this place has to offer.

Integration opens doors to a world of opportunities. It allows one to connect with people from diverse backgrounds, engage in enriching experiences, and contribute meaningfully to the vibrant tapestry of British society. Whether it's participating in local community events, volunteering for worthy causes, or simply striking up conversations with neighbours, there's a sense of fulfilment that comes from being an active and integrated member of the community.

Moreover, the UK presents an abundance of opportunities to enjoy life to the fullest. From its rich history and cultural landmarks to its bustling cities and serene countryside, there is always something new to explore and discover. Whether it's indulging in traditional British cuisine, or taking leisurely strolls along picturesque landscapes, the possibilities for enjoyment are endless.

Integration is a challenging process that requires courage and resilience. It often feels like starting anew, where one must be willing to learn from the ground up, like a child exploring the world for the first time. Immersing oneself in a new language is a key aspect of integration, where every word, accent, and pronunciation may feel unfamiliar.

Integration is a complex process that goes beyond simply learning a new language. It involves adjusting mindsets, embracing new cultural norms, and understanding social nuances. This requires re-evaluating beliefs and being open to different perspectives. One of the most rewarding aspects is the opportunity to engage with individuals from diverse backgrounds, fostering empathy and appreciating cultural diversity.

In essence, integration is a journey of growth and transformation, involving acquiring new skills and shedding old ways of thinking. It entails building connections, bridging cultural divides, and creating a shared sense of community. While challenging, the rewards of integration are vast, offering new experiences, friendships, and a deeper understanding of the world. Integration requires courage to embark on a path of self-discovery and embrace the unknown, ultimately leading to a greater appreciation of cultural richness.

My journey of integration into English culture has been a rollercoaster of emotions and challenges. There's a deep sense of nostalgia for home, a longing for the familiar, and a bittersweet feeling of leaving behind years of experiences and connections. This homesickness can tug at the heartstrings, especially when faced with the initial unfamiliarity of a new environment.

However, amidst this wave of emotions, there's a realisation that this new chapter offers vast opportunities for personal growth. It presents a chance to dive into a different world, unlock hidden potentials, and explore uncharted territories for professional and personal development. The thought of immersing myself in a new culture is both nerve-wracking and thrilling, as it promises a doorway to adventures that may have been beyond reach in my homeland.

However, it is undeniable that the integration process is challenging and can be overwhelming. There are moments where one may feel isolated and lonely, navigating a foreign culture, adapting to unfamiliar norms, and establishing a presence in a new social and professional environment requires a significant amount of mental and emotional strength. The struggle to master a new language, understand cultural subtleties, and assimilate into a different professional world can be exhausting. Despite these challenges, resilience emerges, a resilience fuelled by a deep-seated determination to not just survive but thrive in this new world. It's about striking a delicate balance between staying true to one's roots and embracing the transformations demanded by integration. Ultimately, the journey of integration is a deeply personal odyssey marked by highs and lows, successes, and setbacks. It demands patience, an open attitude, and a willingness to venture beyond one's comfort zone. It's an expedition of self-discovery, where one not only learns about the nuances of a new culture but also unearths strengths, conquers weaknesses, and forges a fresh identity within the diverse and dynamic tapestry of English culture. While the road to integration may be challenging, the fruits of this experience are invaluable. It's about constructing bridges between different worlds, cultivating relationships with individuals from various backgrounds, and contributing to the vibrant mosaic of English society.

The Challenges of Integration

One of the biggest challenges I've faced is forming meaningful connections with people is a lack of skills and cultural understanding. For instance, when it comes to expressing sympathy during times of bereavement and other significant occasions. This is especially crucial for me, given my profound interest in people and my pastoral responsibilities. Communicating effectively in a new environment can often feel like solving a complex puzzle. You're constantly grappling with uncertainty, unsure if your words truly convey your thoughts and feelings, which leads to a lot of second-guessing. Instead of simply being present in the moment, you find yourself constantly strategizing on how to articulate things just right, navigating with an entirely new set of social norms and customs.

For instance, in Eritrea, the customary response to loss involves visiting the grieving family, preparing meals, and offering companionship during the mourning period. Conversely, in the UK, traditions typically include sending flowers or a condolence card and respecting the bereaved need for privacy while grieving.

Reflecting on these cultural distinctions, I recognize instances where I may have struggled to effectively convey my emotions in a way that aligns with British customs during times of loss.

Forming friendships can often be a complex experience, especially when navigating different cultural norms. In Eritrea, there is a strong sense of community that naturally fosters connection and a feeling of equality among individuals. The direct and bold communication style of Eritreans, while sincere, can sometimes be misconstrued as rudeness. On the other hand, in England, there is an emphasis on politeness that can occasionally come off as insincere. Striking a balance between genuine confidence and respectful communication can be a delicate task, as there is a constant concern about unintentionally causing offence due to unfamiliar customs.

As I reflect on my interactions in England, I have come to understand the importance of being authentic while also being mindful of cultural sensitivities. Balancing honesty with tact allows for genuine connections to be formed without compromising one's true self. It is crucial to approach relationships with wisdom, knowing when to express one's thoughts and when to exercise restraint.

Navigating the professional world in a new culture can also present challenges, as biases and preferences can inadvertently impede progress. Building trust and forging meaningful connections take time and effort, particularly when assimilating into a community that may initially perceive you as an outsider. Despite the frustrations that may arise, adapting to a new culture ultimately offers opportunities for growth and fresh perspectives that can enrich your personal experience and contribute to a deeper understanding between communities.

Ultimately, successful integration requires a willingness from both sides to embrace differences and work towards mutual understanding. By serving as a bridge between cultures, individuals can showcase the beauty of diversity and promote unity through acceptance and respect. Integration, when approached with passion and commitment, can lead to harmonious coexistence, and create an environment where the strengths and weaknesses of each culture are acknowledged and appreciated. It is through this mutual respect and appreciation that a sense of belonging and shared understanding can be fostered, enriching both individuals and communities alike.

Developing Genuine Fellowship

I recall that shortly after moving to Huddersfield, my family and I visited 611 Asylum Work, which is a support centre in Huddersfield for refugees and asylum seekers that is run by Elim Pentecostal Church. We were in the process of registering our children for a new primary school and Andrew Lockett, who was working as a volunteer there, offered to assist us and walk us through the registration process step by step. After a few days had passed, I ran into Andrew when I was in the main part of the town. I was excited to meet him, and I invited him to join me for coffee. I insisted that we do things the Eritrean way, which means that since I invited him it was my responsibility to pay for his coffee. He expressed interest in complying with this request. He laughed it off but ultimately conceded that I could pay for it.

It was a great conversation and I got to know him better as a result. Both Andrew and Susan, his wife, and their daughter, Anjali are the most wonderful people I have ever met. It didn't take long for them to become some of my dearest friends among my circle of acquaintances. We always mention them in our family for their kindness. Perhaps this is one of the benefits of integration, making a meaningful connection and building a strong relationship could produce a blessing.

I will be eternally grateful to them for everything they have done for my family and me, and I place a great deal of value on their genuine friendship, counsel, and support. During one of our conversations,

Andrew made the remark that he was attempting to fill the role of a father figure in my life because I had never had one when I was growing up. I was able to feel the genuine care and compassion that he exuded through his words because they were so empathetic and friendly. That was, without doubt, one of the most thoughtful things anyone has ever said to me. My children have formed positive associations with them because of the many occasions on which we have been welcomed into their stunning home over the years.

Opportunities Beyond Elim

Elim Huddersfield has proven to be a gateway to a multitude of opportunities for my ministry. Through their support and connections, I have been able to reach out to various church communities and fellowships, such as the Farsi fellowship led by Maryam and Omid, as well as a Pakistani fellowship with Kaleem and Azam.

These experiences have taught me the importance of staying humble and striving for excellence in all that I do. Additionally, I have had the chance to share my story and experiences at universities in Huddersfield and Leeds, as well as high schools in Bradford and Brighouse, which has been truly enriching.

I have also been able to further my studies at Regents Theological College, thanks to the support and funding provided by Elim Huddersfield. The experience of studying in Malvern has been nothing short of sensational, and I am grateful for the opportunities that have come my way.

I am also thankful for the contributions towards my studies from individuals such as Claire Johnson, Hazel Queening, and Andrew Locket, who have been instrumental in helping me develop my skills. The generosity of the Eritrean family, Sam and Rachel, who have generously donated towards my books, is truly heart-warming. They have even opened a vegetarian restaurant called 'Corarima' in Wakefield, which I highly recommend visiting.

Overall, the integration with Elim Huddersfield has opened up a world of possibilities for my ministry, and I am excited to see where this journey will take me next.

The Tragedy of Lampedusa

The tragic shipwreck off the coast of Lampedusa in 2013 shocked the world and left my wife and me deeply saddened and disturbed. Most of the passengers on the ill-fated boat were refugees from Eritrea, a country close to our hearts. The news hit us hard, bringing back memories of our own journey along that same perilous route.

With the support of Elim Church and the organisation Release Eritrea, I travelled to meet the survivors of the disaster, offering them encouragement and financial aid. During my time there, I had the privilege of connecting with remarkable individuals such as Piero Favara, a retired Italian pastor, Amanuel Debesai, an Eritrean pastor from Germany, and the kind-hearted couple Roberto Recupero and Rosa Alba. I would like to express my gratitude and appreciation about the Recupero family, their kindness was beyond measure. Their house was open to the refugees, they were assisting them with food and encouragement.

The situation in Lampedusa was a scene of heart-wrenching chaos. Families had travelled from across Europe in search of answers about their missing loved ones after the tragic shipwreck. However, the overwhelming demand for information made it difficult for the already strained police to provide the necessary support.

Desperate cries and anguished wails filled the air as families pleaded to see the bodies of their missing relatives. It was a harrowing sight as siblings searched frantically for each other, hoping against hope for a miracle. The emotional intensity of the moment was palpable, leaving a lasting impression on all who witnessed it.

Despite the overwhelming sorrow and pain that hung heavy in the air, we stood by the grieving families for hours on end, offering whatever comfort and solace we could in the face of such unimaginable loss. It was a test of strength and compassion, a moment that etched itself into our memories as a poignant reminder of the fragility of life and the resilience of the human spirit.

After assisting with interpretation for the BBC during an interview with a man who had lost his daughter, the journalist inquired about the reason for my presence in Lampedusa. To summarise, I shared my personal journey from Eritrea to England. This eventually led to a series of interviews and speaking engagements, including appearances at the European Parliament, British Parliament, and the BBC.

Upon returning to England, I found myself invited to speak at various churches and became involved in the Nehemiah prayer project within the Eritrean community. This project, involving fasting and prayer monthly, inspired me to engage in further community initiatives.

The tragedy served as a catalyst, propelling me to advocate for migrants and refugees, raising awareness of the challenges they face and sharing their stories with a wider audience. Through these experiences, I have been humbled by the opportunity to make a difference and contribute to positive change in the lives of those in need.

Return to Swiss Nile Mission

I had always dreamed of visiting the headquarters of the Swiss Nile Evangelical Mission in Switzerland, a destination that held immense personal significance for me. In 2014, this dream became a reality as Switzerland became the top choice for our family holiday. Located in Knonau, the headquarters, known as Mission Am Nil International, had played a pivotal role in shaping not only my life but the lives of many others.

Upon my arrival, I was filled with a deep sense of longing to connect with the dedicated staff members of the organisation, including Markus Fischer, the director, and Michael Bottiger, the director of Swiss Nile Mission Adi-Quala. Meeting these individuals was a privilege, and I took the opportunity to express my gratitude for the profound impact their organisation had on me. My dear wife and children stood beside me, perhaps not fully grasping the depth of my emotions, but for me, this visit was a culmination of gratitude and admiration.

During our meeting, I presented a specially commissioned artwork by a talented Eritrean artist named Milkias. The artwork depicted my background, featuring a tree bearing fruit with a verse from the Bible, Hebrews 6:10, emphasising the importance of not forgetting the work and love shown to others. I explained that this organisation had planted a seed in my life, which had now blossomed into a tree of growth and impact.

The encounter with the staff at the organisation was moving and encouraging. Initially met with hesitation, our meeting evolved into a heartfelt exchange as they expressed how rarely they saw the direct impact of their work on individuals. Witnessing the tangible change in my life inspired them to continue their mission with renewed vigour.

The sight of vibrant streets bustling with activity, the aroma of delicious Eritrean dishes wafting through the air, and the warm smiles of old friends welcoming us back - all of these experiences combined to make this holiday one that will forever hold a special place in my heart.

The joy of reconnecting with friends whom we have not seen in years, sharing stories and laughter over traditional meals, and exploring the beauty of Eritrea together was truly unforgettable. Each city we visited had its own charm and unique attractions, from the serene lakeside of Vevey to the bustling markets of Clarens, Sion to the historical landmarks of Basel and Sarnen.

It was a time of laughter, love, and shared memories that brought us closer as a family and rekindled the bonds of friendship with those we hold dear. The experience of immersing ourselves in the rich culture and hospitality of Eritrea left us with a feeling of warmth and happiness that will linger long after our holiday has ended.

Overall, this holiday was a truly special and fulfilling experience that filled our hearts with joy and our bellies with delicious food. The memories we made and the connections we renewed will always remind us of the beauty and love that surrounds us, both at home and abroad.

As a result of this event, I walked away with a deeper sense of gratitude and a newfound perspective on sacrificial living. The conversations I had with the organisation's leaders about their fundraising efforts were particularly enlightening. Learning about their creative methods, such as crafting candles and growing potatoes to sell, challenged me to think bigger and consider more impactful ways to give back to my own community. This experience has encouraged me to pursue more community activities and embrace a more sacrificial lifestyle, inspired by the selfless work of the Swiss Nile Evangelical Mission.

Launching Joseph Project

The Joseph Project was born out of a powerful encounter in Sudan with Pastor Dr. Kuflu Gebremeskel, whose words struck a chord deep within me. Comparing us to Joseph in the Bible, he likened our persecution by our own brothers to Joseph's own struggles. This resonated strongly as I thought about the plight of those who had fled Eritrea, like Dr. Kuflu himself who was unjustly detained upon his return. As I journeyed to Europe, his message echoed in my mind, highlighting the arduous path of persecution and immigration faced by refugees. Just as Joseph overcame adversity and rose to prominence, I envisioned a similar future for every refugee - one where they integrate, learn, and ultimately emerge as leaders in their communities. Through the Joseph Project, we aim to provide hope, foster cultural understanding, and cultivate a new generation of leaders who embody integrity and dignity. This vision, inspired by Joseph's story, propels us forward on a mission to empower and uplift those who have been displaced from their homes.

The launch of the Joseph Project in 2017 heralded a pivotal moment in the advocacy for refugee rights and well-being. The project's primary objective is to assist refugees and displaced populations in the United Kingdom and beyond. It garnered widespread support from individuals who offered assistance in various forms. One of the most cherished gifts I received was a remarkable painting by artist David Leek, depicting Joseph on his throne as his brothers approached seeking food. Despite their initial fear, Joseph forgave them, recognizing that while they had intended harm, God had planned for good. This powerful depiction symbolises the project's mission to provide hope and blessings to those in need.

My involvement in the project enabled me to visit refugee camps in Ethiopia, Kenya, and Uganda. Many individuals played a crucial role in supporting the project with their unwavering commitment, which included practical, psychological, and spiritual assistance, all of which was truly remarkable. Additionally, Eritrean professionals from various fields offered their support to inspire the refugees to endure persecution, overcome their challenges, and emerge as future leaders within their communities and beyond.

One key aspect of the Joseph Project's impact lies in its engagement with policymakers and influential figures. By speaking at various churches, on mainstream media platforms, and to government officials in Ethiopia, Uganda, and the UK, the project has been able to raise awareness and advocate for refugee rights on a broader scale. These interactions have provided a platform to shape policies, offer valuable perspectives, and champion the cause of refugees within decision-making circles.

Furthermore, the project's engagement with prominent individuals, such as the Archbishop of York, Dr. John Sentamu, has allowed for the sharing of experiences and insights on providing pastoral care and support to refugee communities. These meetings have facilitated important dialogues on the challenges faced by refugees and the importance of upholding fundamental freedoms, such as the freedom of worship.

By leveraging opportunities to engage with policymakers, media outlets, and influential figures, the Joseph Project is not only raising awareness but also driving tangible change in the support and advocacy for refugees. Through education, dialogue, and collaboration, the project is building a platform for refugees to be heard, understood, and empowered in their pursuit of a better future.

Launching the Joseph Leadership Academy

The establishment of the Joseph Leadership Academy in 2019 has brought about remarkable results in the training and development of future leaders within the Eritrean community. Recognizing the untapped potential within these communities, the academy was created with the aim of providing individuals with the necessary skills and guidance to excel in leadership roles.

Through the launch of the online academy, made possible with the invaluable assistance of Natalino Giovanni and Hewan Abraha, the platform has been able to reach a wide audience and offer training opportunities to aspiring leaders from around the world. Additionally, the generous contributions and guidance from Reverend Okbaselassie and Dr. Sirak have played a vital role in the success and growth of the academy.

The impact of the Joseph Leadership Academy is evident in the number of students it has trained, with over 650 individuals benefiting from its programs and resources since its inception. This achievement stands as a testament to the dedication and commitment of all those involved in supporting and nurturing the growth of these emerging leaders.

The rapid growth and success of the academy would not have been possible without the contributions and support of these dedicated individuals. Their generosity and belief in the mission of the academy have paved the way for the development of a new generation of influential leaders who are equipped to make a positive impact in their communities and beyond. The Joseph Leadership Academy continues to strive towards its goal of empowering and inspiring individuals to realise their full potential and contribute meaningfully to society.

In the pursuit of expanding the impact of the Joseph Project, I embarked on a journey filled with invaluable experiences and connections. By heeding the generous invitations of friends to countries such as Israel, Poland, Ethiopia, and Uganda, I was able to delve into a world of learning and growth like never before.

QUESTIONS AND SELF-REFLECTION FOR PRACTICAL STEPS

Question 1

What lessons have you learned from this chapter?

Question 2

Look around you and identify an opportunity to be of help to someone.

Question 3

What new lessons are there for you to learn presently? State them.

Question 4

What price are you willing to pay to achieve excellence in what you do every day?

Question 5

What do you think being great means?

Chapter 7

THE ART OF OVERCOMING THE WILDERNESS

The wilderness may not always be physical, but it manifests itself in different forms and sizes, testing our resilience and strength. Through my own journey, I have learned that the wilderness is a place of growth, transformation, and self-discovery. It is a space where we are confronted with our deepest fears, insecurities, and uncertainties, but also where we can find the courage, determination, and guidance to navigate through the challenges that come our way.

I am no expert, but I have been through my own share of wilderness experiences, from spiritual battles to personal traumas, and I am grateful for the lessons and blessings that have emerged from those trials. I am here to offer my hand to those who are currently facing their own wilderness, to provide support, guidance, and empathy as they journey through the unknown terrain of their lives. Together, we can overcome the obstacles, find our way out of the darkness, and emerge stronger, wiser, and more resilient than ever before.

Let us embrace the wilderness of life with open hearts, knowing that it is a necessary and transformative part of our journey, and that with faith, perseverance, courage, we can emerge victorious on the other side.

I consider myself incredibly blessed to have overcome challenges and reached where I am today. While there are still obstacles ahead, reflecting on my journey has shown me the importance of acknowledging the progress I have made. The principles that have guided me - embracing challenges, trusting in a higher power, finding courage, forgiveness, sharing my story, and believing in my abilities - have been instrumental in my success. I encourage you to adopt these principles to overcome your own challenges. In the following paragraphs, I will share how I navigated certain circumstances and the lessons learned, hoping that you can draw inspiration from my story. By staying true to these guiding principles, you can navigate life's wilderness with resilience and a positive outlook, emerging stronger and more fulfilled.

Trusting in God

I place my trust in God, as I believe in His ability to transform chaos into something good, irrespective of the circumstances. It is through His mercy and provision that my life has been reshaped, becoming a source of encouragement for others. Though uncertainty often clouded my path, the Lord graciously turned my traumatic experiences into meaningful lessons, instilling in me unwavering confidence in facing the future.

My trust in God has evolved as a relational journey, developing gradually over time. From my upbringing steeped in spiritual teachings and the resonance of prophetic songs, a sense of deep trust in the divine has blossomed within me. I vividly recall the resonating melodies sung during nightly gatherings at boarding school, with one hymn holding a special place in my heart. These songs, extolling God's goodness, and enduring mercy, reverberate within me, offering solace and strength in moments of turmoil.

The lyrics "Even though my parents have abandoned me, my Heavenly Father watches over me; He will never leave me and forsake me" have become etched in my being, serving as a constant reminder of God's unwavering presence. In times of uncertainty, the image of God enveloping me in His protection and guidance provides solace and reassurance, leading me to greener pastures.

Firm in the belief that God orchestrates all things for my good, I find solace in the words of Paul: "and we know that for those who love God all things work together for good, for those who are called according to his purpose" (Romans 8:28). This profound assurance simplifies my experience of joy, grounding me in the knowledge that my future rests securely in God's hands. Such understanding propels me towards embracing faith in God, steering clear of pessimism, complaints, or a demanding demeanour, as I navigate life with a heart filled with gratitude and trust.

Trusting in God and witnessing His goodness first-hand has been instrumental in reshaping my life, empowering me to navigate challenging situations and take risks with unwavering faith, even when faced with uncertainty, akin to the pivotal moments of decision-making in Joseph's journey as recounted in the Bible. As I continue to build a foundation of trust in the divine, I have been privileged to witness God's unwavering faithfulness in my life, emboldening my resolve and guiding me through uncharted territories.

One such instance that stands out vividly in my memory is when we found ourselves stranded in the heart of a desert as our vehicle encountered mechanical issues, halting our journey. The tension and anxiety among our group were palpable, with some on the verge of retreat. In that moment of uncertainty, I rallied the group to maintain faith and look beyond the immediate challenges. Through spoken words of faith and prophetic songs that echoed through the barren landscape, a sense of calm permeated the group, fostering a spirit of trust in God's providence amidst adversity.

The dawn of the following day heralded a glimmer of hope as our driver announced the miraculous restoration of our vehicle, allowing us to resume our expedition with renewed vigour and gratitude. This experience underscored the necessity of unwavering faith in God, as it not only pleases Him but also imparts the strength to persevere, aligning our steps with His divine guidance and principles. It is in these moments of unwavering faith that God often leads us toward our purpose, bypassing the intricacies of the unknown with the assurance of His presence.

The poignant tale of Joseph serves as a compelling example of unwavering faith in action, as he embarked on a tumultuous journey marked by unforeseen challenges and trials, ultimately rising to a position of great influence in Egypt. Despite enduring betrayal, slavery, and imprisonment, Joseph clung to his faith in God, showcasing resilience, integrity, and an unshakeable belief in divine faithfulness throughout his arduous path.

Joseph's narrative serves as a testament to the transformative power of trust in God's plan, especially in the face of insurmountable odds and uncertainties. By mirroring Joseph's unwavering faith, we are reminded that aligning our trust with God's promises can furnish us with the tenacity and courage needed to navigate life's hurdles and fulfil our God-given destinies. Just as Joseph's unwavering faith propelled him to a position of influence and purpose, our individual journeys of faith can ultimately lead us to successful journeys.

How did I develop Trust in God?

Trust can be one of the most challenging issues we face in this world. It demands faithfulness, loyalty, and the ability to keep promises. However, once trust is established, it can become one of the most valuable assets in our lives. For example, it can be difficult to trust strangers, which is why having trustworthy friends who can vouch for them makes it easier to extend that trust.

In a similar way, we can trust in God through His only begotten Son, Jesus Christ. When we look at Jesus, we see the epitome of kindness, sacrifice, and friendship. He introduced us to His Father in the best possible way so that we could trust Him wholeheartedly. By following the example set by Jesus, we can build a deep and lasting trust in God, knowing that He always has our best interests at heart.

Trust must be nurtured in accordance with God's word and principles. Romans 10:17 states, "So faith comes from hearing, and hearing through the word of Christ." Contrary to common belief, faith is not based on physical sight but on spiritual perception. Personally, my unwavering belief in God is what empowers me to endure through hardships, to see beyond my immediate circumstances, and to appreciate the blessings in every aspect of my life.

During our perilous fifteen-day journey, we were eventually captured and imprisoned by military personnel in Libya. It was during this time that a man named Daniel approached me, questioning why we were facing yet another trial after all the hardships we had already endured.

He challenged me on why I still trust in God. While I didn't have all the answers, I knew that the jail cell we found ourselves in was merely a temporary resting place, a spot to shake off the dust from our shoes. In that challenging situation, we made a conscious decision to make the most of our time by singing and putting our trust in God. I remember that when we sang daily every morning, "The joy of the Lord became our source of strength amidst the darkness.".

In those moments, I remembered the words of Jeremiah 29:11, which declare, "For I know the plans I have for you, declares the LORD, plans for welfare and not for evil, to give you a future and a hope." This verse from the book of Jeremiah in the Old Testament resonated deeply with me during my time of confinement, providing a sense of meaning and purpose in the midst of our circumstances. Trusting in God's plans and finding solace in His promises allowed us to endure with hope and strength. It served as a reminder that our future was secure and inspired us to focus on finding joy even in the darkest times.

Courage

Courage is not the absence of fear,

but the triumph over it.

—

Nelson Mandela

Overcoming fear and cultivating a positive mental attitude is essential for paving a prosperous path for oneself in the future. Your mindset can significantly impact the quality of your life, despite it seeming trivial. I vividly remember the day I realised I had a choice: to succumb to weakness due to my circumstances or to find strength to overcome them. I chose the latter. However, maintaining strength becomes much more challenging when one harbours a mentality of weakness. Renowned motivational speaker Zig Ziglar once aptly said, "Your attitude determines your altitude," emphasising the critical importance of possessing the right mindset in various aspects of our lives. In hindsight, I wish I had grasped this concept sooner and opted to adopt a more resilient and determined attitude.

Solomon, the wisest king of Israel, is credited with saying in Proverbs 23:7, "As a man thinks, so he is." Our thoughts and hearts shape our character and reveal our true selves, especially when faced with difficulties. It is crucial to realise that, regardless of our current position in life, we are deserving of and possess the potential to achieve great things. Even in discouraging circumstances, one can instil faith that with effort, things will improve over time. Continuous self-criticism leads to the development of a negative and defeatist mindset. Instead, striving to maintain a positive outlook and an open mind can help improve one's situation.

It is possible to learn and develop courage by adjusting your fundamental belief system. While we may not be able to eliminate the natural feeling of fear, we should not let it prevent us from doing the right thing, which is having courage in the face of difficult situations. Some individuals may naturally have a positive attitude, while others may need to train their minds to think more positively. Regardless, maintaining the right attitude is crucial.

I used to struggle with fear, shyness, and fragility when I was younger, making it hard for me to face the unknown or speak up for myself. Over time, I have become more resilient and have adopted a more optimistic outlook. For example, when a child was born while we were travelling through the Mediterranean Sea, everyone had the opportunity to celebrate, but some passengers seemed frozen with fear, overshadowing the joy. However, with courage, we can still celebrate even in challenging circumstances.

Fear can be contagious and quickly spread, making it dangerous in remote areas. However, having courage helps us overcome any wilderness circumstances. So, I have learned that no matter how daunting the situation, we should remain courageous, stay strong, and trust that things will work out for the best with faith in God.

While people can survive without food and water for a certain amount of time, living without hope is incredibly challenging. This lack of hope is often a contributing factor to individuals contemplating suicide, as they see no positive outlook for the future. But what exactly is hope? Hope involves trusting that God will reward us for our efforts, and it is not just wishful thinking but a belief system that motivates us to take meaningful action.

When one is hopeful, they constantly imagine and visualise positive outcomes, which serves as inspiration to actively pursue their goals. In today's world, it is essential to have hopeful individuals who can bring about positive changes in various circumstances. Hope is not merely a passive feeling, but a guiding force that propels us to envision a better future and work towards making it a reality.

I understand that facing difficult circumstances is not easy; I have personally experienced the challenges of navigating through the wilderness. It's in these tough moments that it becomes tempting to lose hope. However, giving in to despair and doing nothing will only make the situation worse. On the other hand, maintaining hope can inspire action and create positive changes.

For example, when our boat collided with a larger vessel in the Mediterranean Sea, causing a puncture that led to water leaking into our small boat, many lost hopes in our journey to Italy. People doubted our chances of making it, which led to a lack of cooperation in bailing out the water. Despite our efforts to motivate them, some individuals remained apathetic, claiming they didn't care. It became evident that losing hope resulted in passivity instead of proactive problem-solving.

Therefore, it's crucial to remain hopeful and encouraged, holding onto the belief that circumstances can be changed for the better. By visualising a brighter tomorrow and maintaining a high level of hope, we can navigate through challenging times and work towards a positive outcome. As the Apostle Paul urges us in Romans chapter 12, we should "rejoice in hope" because hope has the power to sustain us through difficult moments.

Healing from the Past

"If you never heal from what hurt you, you'll bleed on people who didn't cut you." Tamara Kulish

This poignant statement resonates with many, highlighting the importance of healing from past wounds. But how does one go about healing? The key lies in understanding and finding meaning in our past experiences. Those who have healed from their past pain often go on to positively impact the future.

Take the story of Joseph, for example. Despite being persecuted by his own brothers, sold into slavery, and wrongly accused and imprisoned, he found purpose and forgiveness. Instead of harbouring resentment, he chose to uplift and positively influence those around him.

Joseph's journey serves as a powerful lesson on the possibility of healing from past wounds and moving forward with grace and positivity.

It shows us that through forgiveness and finding meaning, we too can overcome our past traumas.

Reflecting on my childhood, I have realised that life's journey often throws difficult challenges our way. There were moments when circumstances felt unjust, leaving me hurt and confused. While I can't change the past or the circumstances I was born into, I've learned that dwelling on what could have been serves no purpose.

I understand that my experiences are just a small part of the broader human suffering tapestry. Many individuals face much greater hardships than I have ever known. Despite this, I have discovered healing and resilience within my own journey. Through introspection and personal growth, I have emerged from tough times stronger and more compassionate.

Today, I find comfort in the belief that my experiences can serve a higher purpose. I feel privileged to have shared my story in various settings, resonating with many who have found comfort and encouragement through it. It is through my healing journey and self-discovery that I have found meaning and purpose in my past struggles.

The journey to healing may be slow, but addressing certain issues is key to making progress. Personally, I believe that recognizing the depth of my emotional state without resentment is crucial.

Many of the wounds I carry were influenced by circumstances beyond my control, such as the death of my family, actions of authorities over me, natural disasters, and political situations. While I may not have control over these events, I do have control over how I choose to respond. I can either dwell on negative feelings or entrust my cares to God, who has the power to turn any situation around (1 Pet 5:7).

Though I couldn't prevent the circumstances that led to my wounds, I could control my reaction by choosing forgiveness and establishing boundaries. This mindset has guided me on the path to healing, enabling me to manage my emotions and avoid unnecessary bitterness.

I remember a particular occasion when I was invited to share my story around a campfire, encircled by a group of friends. The crackling flames illuminated the setting, casting a warm glow as our narratives unfolded, interweaving a tapestry of connection and empathy among the audience. This act of storytelling is akin to a mystical thread that binds us together, drawing us closer through vulnerability and understanding. It holds the transformative power to emancipate individuals. Upon concluding my account, a friend rose and confided, "I harbour a similar story that I've carried for years. Now, feeling liberated, I am determined to share my story without shame, recognizing its potential to free others."

Indeed, sharing demands courage. It involves laying bare your innermost self to the world, showcasing all its imperfections and scars.

While critics and detractors may seek to dull your radiance, there exist numerous individuals awaiting eagerly to uplift you. The act of vulnerability not only fosters personal healing but also sets off a chain reaction of emotional recovery in those who resonate with your journey. The benefits are reciprocal for both the storyteller and those who find solace and empowerment in shared narratives.

Envision this ripple effect expanding outward, touching hearts, and igniting dialogues that dissolve barriers of solitude and shame. Your story serves as a guiding light, leading others out of shadows towards the illumination of common experiences. Through the exchange of giving and receiving, of listening and narrating, genuine bonds are forged that transcend obstacles of age, race, and upbringing.

Therefore, embrace the inherent strength in sharing your story. Let your voice resonate, your truth unfolds, and your heart unfurl. Within the act of sharing resides the magic of connectivity and rejuvenation – a force capable of transforming not only your own existence but also of those in your vicinity. Sharing necessitates an embrace of vulnerability and fortitude. This action not only aids in emotional processing but also nurtures connections with individuals encountering similar challenges. Through these exchanges, I have come to appreciate the vitality of empathy and the therapeutic potential of communal experiences. Despite the possibility of encountering those who may not relate or respond insensitively, embracing vulnerability with a receptive audience can facilitate the journey towards healing from pain. I firmly believe that such actions have contributed significantly to my mental well-being. Cultivating inner peace and contributing to the lives of others amplify joy. Walking a purposeful path shapes expectations, potentially leading to a sound mental health foundation.

Emotional Wellbeing

The perilous journey through the Sahara and Mediterranean Sea, combined with parental absence and traumatic experiences, can inflict profound emotional wounds on individuals, leading to a cascade of negative effects on their emotional well-being. The absence of parental figures can leave children feeling abandoned, unworthy, and devoid of emotional support, fostering self-hatred and deep-seated insecurity. Similarly, experiences of abuse, neglect, or exposure to violence can shatter one's sense of safety and trust, plunging them into a state of hopelessness and despair. This destructive combination often results in self-destructive behaviours and a pervasive belief that life lacks meaning or value, ultimately heightening the risk of suicide as a perceived escape from relentless suffering. Research underscores the significant impact of parental absence during childhood on mental health and behavioural issues. Parental care in early childhood is pivotal for nurturing both cognitive and emotional development in children. Parents and caregivers play crucial roles in helping children cope emotionally and develop behaviourally by offering positive reinforcement, love, respect, and instilling confidence. When this nurturing presence is absent or disrupted, children may struggle with managing their emotions and relationships, making them vulnerable to various psychological challenges that can persist into adulthood.

I am deeply grateful for the blessings I have received in life. Despite the challenges I have faced, I believe I have emerged as a person with robust emotional, spiritual, mental, and physical well-being. I am thankful for the physical strength and resilient character I have developed over time, even though my children might humorously contest that perspective. Reflecting on my upbringing, marked by the loss of four family members in childhood and growing up without the warmth of a traditional family setting, compounded by experiences such as enduring regimes, crossing treacherous borders, traversing the unforgiving Sahara Desert, and facing the perils of imprisonment and dangerous sea crossings, I acknowledge the potential impact these adversities could have had on my mental health and emotional resilience. Having encountered numerous testimonies from individuals who share similar backgrounds to mine, I am acutely aware of the struggles that many face in navigating life after such traumatic experiences. The haunting flashbacks and persistent trauma often cast a long shadow, making it challenging for them to find peace or solace in their daily existence. Frustration, anger, and even tendencies toward violence become familiar companions, overshadowing any semblance of joy or contentment. Simple activities that most take for granted can become fraught with emotional landmines; for instance, the mere sight of a swimming pool can evoke visceral memories of the perilous journey across

For example, catching a glimpse of a swimming pool might unexpectedly trigger intense memories of the treacherous journey across the Mediterranean Sea, unleashing a torrent of anxiety and fear. These individuals often feel ensnared by their past, unable to shake off the chains of trauma that loom over every aspect of their lives. However, even in the depths of despair, a glimmer of hope remains that, with unwavering support and resilience, they can gradually break free from the grasp of their past and rediscover the beauty that surrounds them.

It is a truly humbling experience to attempt to grasp the profound suffering endured by these individuals. Truthfully, I too have moments where I grapple with my own inner demons, albeit infrequently. One of the most haunting dreams I have is transported back to my boarding school days, innocently playing, only to be viciously attacked by the school director, sending me crashing to the ground. The shock of waking from such nightmares leaves me disoriented, yet grateful to find safety in my bed. Another chilling dream whisks me back to Eritrea, where I am relentlessly pursued by military police, consumed by regret forever leaving.

Desperation drives me to flee across the border, only to be met with the deafening roar of gunfire, abruptly snapping me out of deep sleep. In those jarring moments of awakening, surrounded by the comfort of my home and loved ones in England, a wave of relief and security washes over me. These glimpses into the shadowy recesses of my subconscious serve as poignant reminders of the value of safety and the sanctity of home.

Driven by profound empathy and a desire to offer hope, I share my personal journey, acknowledging the struggles faced by many Eritrean individuals due to their backgrounds and traumatic experiences. This compels me to illuminate a path of resilience and renewal for those who may feel lost in the darkness. I was privileged to be invited for a tour in the United States last year, engaging with Eritrean communities and their second generation, openly sharing my experiences. The response was heartening, as many found solace and inspiration in my words, sparking conversations about healing and empowerment within families and communities. From counselling sessions to mentoring emerging leaders, I have endeavoured to instil hope and possibility, actively contributing to positive change in our society.

To my surprise, I have received humbling compliments from friends, colleagues, and individuals in both the UK and Eritrea who have benefited from my counselling and the services I provide to help them overcome challenges. Those who know me well, such as my friend John Alula, are amazed at the grace they perceive in me. John once remarked, "It's hard to believe that you have a difficult background," as he sees me as a confident and positive person. On another occasion, my good friend Reverend Mark Stone complimented me by saying,

"Your one-on-one counselling is excellent." This sentiment resonates with the biblical saying, "Can anything good come out of Nazareth?" While these acknowledgments touch me deeply, I do not claim these accomplishments as my own; rather, I attribute them to the grace of God, my Lord and Shepherd, who has shaped my journey.

Perhaps my contribution lies in simply accepting the reality of my humble beginnings and trusting that the Lord can use them for His glory. If Jesus could turn water into wine, I believe that an ordinary life can be transformed into something extraordinary and useful.

Understanding Your Journey

Some individuals are born into privilege, such as wealth or royal families, providing them with unique opportunities, resources, and social status from the outset. While this reality may seem unfair to some, it is essential to appreciate the advantages that come with such circumstances. Growing up with abundant resources and influential connections can open doors that can be hard to come by for others. However, my journey started humbly. Yet, this does not mean that my life will always remain the same. I have realised that life presents various paths, each with its own challenges and opportunities. While some may begin with privilege, others, like myself, start from more modest beginnings. I've come to understand that the beauty of life lies in its diversity and unpredictability. Challenges, no matter how daunting, can serve as catalysts for personal growth and resilience. It is through facing adversity that we discover our inner strength and capacity for endurance. Despite the struggles, we may sometimes lose sight of the blessings that come with humble beginnings. It is easy to fall into the trap of comparison and focus solely on what we lack. Instead, embracing challenges and beginnings, no matter how small, can lead to significant personal growth and a deeper appreciation for the journey ahead.

The temptation to envy others, particularly those who appear to have more fortune or privilege, can be strong, leading us to overlook the opportunities we must make meaningful contributions. I recall moments when jealousy consumes me, comparing myself unfavourably to those seemingly better off in various aspects of life, even in trivial matters. Letting such feelings take hold was foolish, yet at the time, they caused doubt about my worth and my family's circumstances. Spiralling into self-blame, questioning my perceived shortcomings, left me feeling disheartened and helpless. Today, many people compare their lives with others, especially with the prevalence of social media. Displays of wealth, beauty, and privileges can trigger comparison and peer pressure, leading to discouragement and depression. Over time, I have realised that every challenge I faced has contributed to shaping the person I am today. Each obstacle presented an opportunity for growth and resilience, offering valuable lessons and fortifying my character. Today, I embrace my journey with gratitude, acknowledging that overcoming adversity has revealed my true strength and potential. It is best to focus on the future and move forward, as no matter how you start in life, a brighter future lies ahead.

Sometimes people ask, "How do you manage to settle family conflicts and arguments with all the challenges you faced during the long and arduous journey?" My answer is, as Max Lucado once said, conflict is inevitable, but combat is optional.

Honestly, I feel incredibly blessed to have such a beautiful family, and sometimes I doubt if I truly deserve it. Growing up, I wasn't equipped with the proper experience. I never had the chance to sit down with my parents and discuss different opinions, problem-solving, handle conflicts, but maintain family unity firmly. It wasn't easy managing all of this, especially with the constant travelling and moving from place to place.

I am immensely grateful for my incredible wife, Senayit, whose patience and wisdom surpass any I've encountered. Her steadfast support has been an anchor, particularly amid our frequent travels and the constant flux of our family life with the children. Juggling finances and the demands of my ministry and community service often take me away from home, yet Senayit remains an unwavering source of assistance and strength. Her contributions are invaluable and undeniable, shaping our journey with grace and resilience.

However, even with her wonderful qualities, when she's angry, her fiery eyes and demeanour can be intimidating. So, looking back, we had some serious conflicts on our journey.

Obviously, there are personal and perspective differences. I'm a kind of risk-taker, which means I sometimes quickly jump into things. Sometimes it helps, but other times it doesn't. Whereas my wife is a completely different person, very contemplative, slow to action. I can confess that because of my quick decisions, I've made some mistakes, which is humiliating. I hope that on this issue, I've learned to listen and consult with my wife; I think this is wisdom. On the other hand, there were times when we delayed taking action, and it could have been productive, but because of extreme caution, we didn't take action. I hope that my wife learned the needed lesson as well. It is about respecting, understanding, and valuing each other and maintaining balance.

So, after many conflicts, I have learned to discuss the issue openly, to negotiate while remaining true to my values but flexible on the methods.

For instance, let me share where my wife and I used to have conflicts quite often. Whenever I had the opportunity to speak about my journey in a newspaper or on TV channels, most agencies requested a family photo, but my wife was not keen to do that. At first, I didn't understand why she felt this way. I thought she was afraid, or she didn't want to stand up for others. However, her intention was the best—to keep our family out of the public eye. Being in the public eye could attract so many unnecessary tensions to our family. So, we had arguments over this, sometimes involving the whole family, leading to a cold silence in the house.

I've learned that being flexible and understanding the perspectives of others is crucial and the importance of family protection. However, on the other hand, using the platform to bring hope to those who feel hopeless and shed light on justice-related issues is a huge opportunity. Both perspectives are valid, so we needed to find the right balance.

Finally, we decided to agree on speaking the truth without including a family photo, allowing us to achieve both of our goals. I agreed and took swift action immediately. I remember calling the news agency to cancel and remove the news and our family photo from their post. The news agent responded kindly and understood the situation. She commented, "This is a lovely story and a lovely photo," but I insisted on its removal. Another newspaper requested an interview with a family photo as a must, so I simply declined their offer. So, this is how we manage by remaining true to our values and flexible on the methods.

Having said that, I'm still learning how to resolve conflicts, which is a lifelong commitment. My favourite strategy is choosing the right time for negotiation, as it makes a big difference. Creating a favourable atmosphere could make the negotiation workable. I usually bring up the issue during a wonderful coffee celebration when everyone is laughing and enjoying themselves. Choosing the right time can significantly decrease the intensity of arguments, unnecessary words, and solve conflicts easily, which most of the time, I win. One time, I remember my wife said, 'I'm not going to have a conversation to solve an issue over a coffee ceremony.' I asked why? She responded, 'Because you always win, I think you're gifted at talking!' I laughed... So, sometimes our conflicts turn into laughter, which is great. When we pick the opportune moment to address concerns or discuss sensitive topics, it often leads to more productive and constructive conversations. Because during that time the heart is ready, the mind is sharp, and the words are smoother.

Moreover, considering the right time means considering each family member's schedule and mood. Engaging in discussions when everyone is well-rested and not preoccupied with other stressors fosters an environment where everyone feels heard and respected.

By being mindful of timing, we create space for open and healthy communication, ultimately strengthening our family bonds and minimising unnecessary conflicts. Personally, I find that respecting my wife and prioritising the family first helps us on our journey. Instead of "picking a fight," a more effective approach to resolving disagreements within a family setting would be to engage in respectful and constructive communication. This involves actively listening, empathising with others' viewpoints, and expressing one's thoughts and feelings calmly and clearly.

By focusing on understanding rather than "winning," family members can collaborate to find solutions, compromise when necessary, and maintain healthy relationships. It's not about coming out on top but rather about fostering understanding, respect, and harmony within the family unit.

QUESTIONS AND SELF-REFLECTION FOR PRACTICAL STEPS

Question 1

What lessons have you learned from this chapter?

Question 2

What kind of wilderness are you facing at the moment?

Question 3

What principles or lessons will you apply to help you overcome challenges?

Question 4

What do you think is the best way to help others overcome their wilderness?

Question 5

How do your actions align with the hope you have to overcome your current wilderness?

Chapter 8

YOUR GIFT IS YOUR CURRENCY TO EXCELLENCE

I firmly believe that each individual on this planet possesses a unique gift or talent. Unfortunately, many of us unintentionally choose to overlook these inherent capabilities and instead seek something external. We often fall into the trap of believing that the key to self-improvement lies in acquiring new skills rather than honing the ones we already possess.

This concept reminds me of a poignant story from Africa about a man who sold his house to pursue his dream of mining precious stones but tragically lost his life on that quest. Surprisingly, the new owner of his property later discovered a diamond in the backyard after cultivating the land. The precious gem had been there all along, patiently waiting to be unearthed.

Reflecting on this tale, I realised that I, too, had a dormant talent that I hadn't fully explored – singing. Despite my childhood passion for music, I had never considered pursuing a singing career. I was not pro-active in excelling about the gift. Instead of cultivating, polishing, and maximising it, I was just waiting for something to happen in my life.

In fact, I was pursuing something else. After a failed venture to establish a clinic in Addis Ababa, I returned to Keren and decided to focus on nurturing my singing talent by writing songs. An encounter with a church pastor in Asmara who was moved by my performance at a Sunday service sparked a journey of growth and collaboration with musicians. While facing initial humiliation and discouragement from criticism, I persevered and noticed my talent blossoming.

After much dedication and hard work, I completed my first album titled "Greater Love Has No One Than This, Than to Lay Down One's Life for His Friends." The transformative journey of creating this album brought immense joy and fulfilment, leaving me feeling completely renewed. As I listened to the track "I Love You Jesus from the Bottom of My Heart," included on the album, a profound sense of peace washed over me.

The album received widespread acclaim and made a significant financial contribution towards supporting full-time pastors in our church. However, more importantly the experience taught me a vital lesson:

Firstly, I believe it is crucial to appreciate and nurture the talents and abilities I already possess, rather than constantly chasing after new skills. By focusing on developing and applying my existing potential, I can achieve a deeper sense of fulfilment and make a more meaningful impact. Just like gardens, my gifts require careful and consistent cultivation to truly flourish.

Secondly, I should not be afraid to share my talents and abilities, even if they are not perfected. The process of nurturing our gifts can be challenging, especially when we hold high expectations. Waiting for my skills to reach a state of perfection before sharing them can often lead to missed opportunities and unnecessary delays. Instead, I should aim for excellence, continuously striving to improve while also being willing to put myself out there. My imperfect contributions can still have a significant positive impact, and the process of sharing can be a catalyst for growth and refinement.

Thirdly, instead of concentrating on my weaknesses, it is more beneficial to work on my strengths. Dwelling on my weaknesses often leads to disappointment and distracts me from acquiring new talents. Conversely, focusing and developing my strengths provides hope and a sense of contribution to the world. I have learned that by embracing my talents and enhancing my strengths, I can open the door to bigger opportunities and make a more meaningful impact. This approach not only boosts my confidence but also allows me to utilise my unique abilities to their fullest potential.

The journey of creating my first album was instrumental in raising the bar and inspiring tenderization. It brought blessings both fanatically and spiritually to the church. Many solo singers from different churches were encouraged to pursue recording quality, standard albums after recognizing my gift as a currency for excellence in life. Despite facing criticism and challenges, perseverance ultimately led to the completion of my album, "Greater Love Has No One Than This, Than to Lay Down One's Life for His Friends." This marked a transformative journey towards fulfilment and recognition.

In the pursuit of excellence, it is crucial to understand the distinction between excellence and perfection. Striving for excellence entails performing tasks to the best of our abilities, while perfection remains unattainable and may hinder progress. Embracing excellence allows for growth and skill enhancement, fostering a positive mindset that drives continuous improvement. Shifting focus from perfection to excellence eliminates feelings of disillusionment and sustains motivation. By welcoming constructive criticism and discerning its intent, we gather valuable experience from failures, propelling personal development. As we consistently dedicate ourselves to excellence, recognition follows from both ordinary individuals and influential figures.

Our skills and abilities possess the purpose of aiding others, rather than purely for self-aggrandisement. Utilising our talents joyfully in various contexts, like my music in times of need, grants us the potential to make a profound impact. Music has been a source of healing for me, offering a creative outlet to express emotions, undergo cathartic release, and facilitate transformation towards healing. The power of singing transcends the performance, providing solace, inspiration, and blessings in life's trials. Choosing joy over negative emotions can uplift spirits and inspire personal growth, paving the way for resilience and triumph over adversities. Ultimately, pursuing a life of excellence, not perfection, through a spirit of service and dedication offers fulfilment and meaningful success.

Through the intention of this book, firstly, I aim to inspire and uplift all those who have made a difference in someone else's life. Your contributions in assisting others have not gone unnoticed. I am certain that numerous individuals have been positively impacted by your actions, just as I have. Therefore, please take pride in yourself and remain encouraged. Even if you have not received direct feedback on the effects of your efforts, the impact you have made is invaluable.

Secondly, I would like to offer words of encouragement to those facing difficult circumstances, losses, and tragedies in life. I hope that you will find clarity and strength as you navigate through those challenging times. Remember that humble beginnings can be transformed, so please do not give up and stay hopeful.

Thirdly, I would like to encourage individuals to discover and cultivate their gifts as a way to make a positive impact on the world and break away from the ordinary. It is easy for circumstances to make you doubt yourself, but rather than waiting passively, being proactive and determined can lead to significant changes. This determination can serve as a valuable asset in bringing blessings and excellence into your life.

May this book serve as a source of inspiration for you to start something good and leave a lasting impact on the world. Together, we can continue the cycle of kindness and generosity, ensuring that each act of compassion creates a ripple effect of positive change.

QUESTIONS AND SELF-REFLECTION FOR PRACTICAL STEPS

The following questions are intended to stimulate your thinking about the chapter's content and assist you in learning some lessons. Please take some time to reflect and absorb useful information. Consider the story's relevance to your own life experiences, let your mind wander, be encouraged to challenge yourself, and look for ways to make the world a better place.

Question 1

What lessons have you learned from this chapter?

Question 2

Have you identified your gifts and talents?

Question 3

In what ways are you willing to develop these gifts and talents?

Question 4

What principles will you apply to work out these gifts and talents?

Chapter 9

FINDING GREATNESS BY SEEKING VALUES

It appears that the pursuit of greatness is a common aspiration for many individuals, particularly those in influential roles such as politicians, artists, and religious leaders, who often seek fame and power. However, the quest for greatness devoid of values and purpose can lead to a superficial and egotistical lifestyle.

About a decade ago, an individual vying for a leadership position in the church exhibited a misguided pursuit of greatness. Despite his recent membership and youthfulness, he sought to ascend to the role of elder for perceived prestige and access to congregation members. When questioned about his motives, his response cantered on personal gain rather than genuine service. Recognizing the shallowness of his ambition, I advised him against his pursuit. Sadly, in the following years, he veered down a destructive path, ultimately resulting in his dismissal from leadership and departure from the church. This experience underscored that true greatness transcends mere titles, power, or popularity.

Authentic greatness lies in serving others and leading a life that uplifts and transforms others. As Jesus said, "The greatest among you shall be your servant." (Matthew 23:11) By serving others, there is the possibility to turn their void into fulfilment and their wilderness into a valley of water.

Reflecting on my own journey, for me the project runners at the boarding school, Swiss Nile Evangelical Mission, are some of the greatest people. They played an instrumental role in shaping my life. Their provision of refuge and support in the orphanage marked the turning point that paved the way for my growth and development. Their selfless dedication and impact on my life exemplify the essence of greatness. It is often noted that the happiest individuals are those who dedicate themselves to serving others, offering kindness, volunteering, and providing a listening ear to those in need.

The joy derived from making a positive impact in someone else's life, irrespective of scale, is incomparable. Acts of selflessness and compassion not only benefit the recipient but also grant a deep sense of purpose and connectedness. Engaging in service cultivates empathy, gratitude, and understanding, expanding our horizons beyond personal concerns, and fostering a united sense of community well-being.

Moreover, supporting others brings unanticipated blessings and opportunities for personal growth. Through these interactions, we glean insights into resilience, humility, and the significance of human connection. These experiences enrich our lives, nurturing qualities of compassion, resilience, and empathy.

Wealth and popularity should not be defined or measured by material possessions but by the joy and fulfilment derived from serving others. By extending kindness, compassion, and support, we contribute to a collective while fostering our own happiness and well-being. It is important to foster orphans and abandoned children due to various circumstances. Recently, I have been deeply affected by the news of war and unrest in regions like Ukraine, Eritrea, Ethiopia, Tigray, and more. This turmoil often results in parents losing their lives, leaving behind vulnerable orphaned children. This reality resonates with my own childhood experiences.

Through my connections, I have become aware of the plight of numerous children in Eritrea and Northern Ethiopia who find themselves parentless, lost, and with nowhere to turn. Conversely, there are couples yearning for a child but facing biological constraints. I have contemplated the potential of connecting these two groups—the orphans in need of parents and the eager couples—in a harmonious bond, a blessing that could mutually enrich their lives. While this endeavour may not be simple, my personal transformation and hope instil courage in me to dream of such possibilities.

I firmly believe that becoming a guardian or foster parent, even to a child not biologically related, is a profound blessing. It presents an opportunity to offer love, stability, and guidance to a child who may otherwise remain vulnerable. Those with the capacity to open their hearts and homes to these children perform an incredible act of kindness, with rewards that extend to both the child and the caregiver. Drawing from my own experiences at the Swiss Nile Evangelical Mission, I have witnessed first-hand how such care can positively impact vulnerable children, motivating me to pay forward the blessings I received.

Moreover, I aim to inspire individuals, couples, and parents with resources to actively contribute to transforming challenging circumstances into blessings, mirroring the positive impact in my own life. Together, through financial support, volunteering, or raising awareness, each person can make a difference and uplift the lives of these vulnerable children, creating a brighter future for them and our communities at large.

Turning a tragic loss and abandonment into a beacon of hope and opportunity for these young ones is a shared endeavour. I firmly believe that every child deserves a loving home, a nurturing environment, and the chance to reach their full potential.

Desmond Tutu's timeless words, "Your ordinary acts of love and hope point to the extraordinary promise that every human life is of inestimable value," serve as a daily reminder for me to embody love, compassion, and humility. True greatness is not defined by one's position but by the service they provide to others. Pursuing values over glory allows for the cultivation of compassionate leadership and offers hope to those in need.

It would be incredibly impactful if individuals who have been positively influenced and supported by kind-hearted people in their lives choose to pay it forward. This concept of a reverse missionary involves those who have been fostered and cared for, deciding to give back and initiate projects to support and uplift those who have made a difference in their lives.

The idea of reciprocating the goodness they have received by showing appreciation and support to those who have been instrumental in their growth and success is truly magnificent. This reverse act of kindness and service has the power to create a ripple effect of positivity and gratitude, transforming the lives of those who have dedicated themselves to helping others.

Recognizing and honouring the contributions of these influential individuals through initiatives that aim to acknowledge their impact and provide support can foster a sense of collective appreciation and unity. This gesture of gratitude and giving back not only embodies the spirit of reciprocity but also highlights the profound impact of generosity, kindness, and selflessness in building a stronger, more compassionate community.

Ultimately, the act of reversing the goodness received by serving and supporting those who have dedicated themselves to helping others is a beautiful testament to the transformative power of gratitude, compassion, and the enduring legacy of kindness. I am a product of a missionary's influence, and I am here to do whatever is possible to recreate the goodness that has shaped my life, a concept I refer to as a reverse missionary.

Reverse Missionaries & Reconnecting with great people

There is a deep and indescribable sense of joy that comes from giving back to those who have been like heroes in our lives, guiding and supporting us through the ups and downs of our journey. These individuals have been like pillars of strength, standing by us in our darkest moments and guiding us towards the light when all seemed lost.

As I reflect on my unexpected journey to the West, I can't help but feel immense gratitude towards those who have helped me along the way. Their selfless acts of kindness and unwavering support have shaped the path that led me to where I am today.

Meeting and serving those who have been instrumental in our lives is not just a one-way street; it is a mutual blessing. By giving back to our heroes, we not only show our appreciation but also continue the cycle of kindness and support, creating a ripple effect that touches not only our lives but the lives of others as well.

In this journey of giving back, we come to realise that our heroes are not just individuals who have impacted our lives but living examples of how kindness, compassion, and generosity can make a lasting difference in the world. As we pay homage to those who have helped us along the way, we not only honour their contributions but also inspire others to follow in their footsteps, creating a legacy of love and service that transcends time and space.

A Second Journey to Switzerland

Someone once said, "Switzerland is the garden of Eden on Earth." I believe they are correct, as the beauty of the land is truly mesmerising. I have had the opportunity to visit different parts of Switzerland, each one more beautiful than the last.

Last summer, my family and I visited Switzerland, and for me, it holds a special connection that brings back memories of my childhood. The kindness and generosity of the people there played a significant role in transforming my life. While for my family, the natural beauty of the land is simply enjoyable. In fact, my wife even wondered why we hadn't considered moving to Switzerland.

The famous mountain village of Grindelwald is nestled in a unique Alpine landscape that exudes unparalleled beauty. Picture a charming village surrounded by lush meadows and chalet-style houses, all framed by the imposing backdrop of the Eiger north face, where the air is truly invigorating.

The landscape of Vevey offers unforgettable impressions, especially with its picturesque vineyards cascading down to the shores of Lake Geneva. The lakefront provides a panoramic view, making it a perfect spot for a leisurely stroll along the shores. And who can forget the impressive Waterfall of Vernayaz, also known as Pissevache, one of Switzerland's most breath-taking natural wonders? The cascading water creates a captivating spectacle as it plunges into the rocky basin below, blending the roaring water with the serene beauty of the alpine scenery. It brings back memories of the waterfall of 'Adi Keteyo' where I grew up.

However, the feeling of being able to repay the kindness of those who have blessed you is truly something special. The excitement and gratitude that come with serving the very people who have supported and uplifted you on your journey is indescribable.

Imagine my life without the generosity of the Swiss Nile Mission—I wouldn't be where I am today. Their selfless support has enabled me to achieve things I never thought possible. Now, having the opportunity to minister to them and reconnect is simply beautiful.

In 2018, my heart raced with excitement as I was invited to Switzerland to minister and share my story with the very mission that organised the boarding school in Adi-Quala. Accompanied by my dear friend Medhanie, we embarked on this journey with eager anticipation.

Upon arriving at the grand building, I was greeted by a sight that brought tears to my eyes—a massive poster at the entrance emblazoned with my photo and the words "Welcome Daniel Habtey." At that moment, an overwhelming wave of blessings and courage washed over me. It was my turn now, I thought, to give back and serve others.

The warmth and hospitality of the people were truly extraordinary. The program was meticulously organised, and I found myself engaged in a lively Q&A session, where questions flowed about my family, ministry, and plans to visit the boarding school in Eritrea. Each question was filled with genuine curiosity and heartfelt interest.

Then came a question that took me back to nostalgic times: "Can you sing one of the songs you used to sing in boarding school?" I scratched my head, pondering which song to choose, and then, like a lightbulb moment, I remembered a particularly special one. Picking up my guitar, I began to sing, strumming the familiar chords.

To my amazement, as I sang, the entire audience joined in! At first, I was utterly bewildered—how did they know the song? It turned out that the song had been translated into several different languages, allowing everyone to sing along in their own tongue. The atmosphere was nothing short of electric, and in that shared moment of music and unity, I felt an indescribable connection to every person there. It was a truly unforgettable experience that filled my heart with joy and fulfilment.

During my visit, I was also amazed by the innovative ways they generate money to support the boarding school. The simple yet effective methods they employ, such as growing and selling potatoes and creating and selling Christmas cards, showcase their dedication and creativity in giving back to those in need. Their ability to excel in their gifts and talents to make a difference in people's lives is truly inspiring.

As someone whose life has been transformed by their mission, I am a living testament to the impact of their work. I firmly believe that my mission has also positively impacted others and will continue to change lives for the better. Though it may seem like a small start compared to others, the goal remains the same: to make a difference in the lives of others.

Journey to Ethiopia

Embarking on a mission journey to Ethiopia was a life-changing experience, one that will always hold a special place in my heart. With the support of Elim Mission, Release Eritrea, and CAM International, I had the incredible opportunity to impact the lives of refugees in a camp, helping them to plan for a brighter future and develop essential leadership skills.

Visiting a prison cell in Ethiopia was a sobering yet eye-opening experience, where I was able to connect with Eritrean individuals facing incarceration. Sharing personal stories and distributing essential items conveyed a message of resilience and hope conveyed, reminding me of the power of human connection and compassion.

Among the many unforgettable moments of my journey, reconnecting with Masresha Gebremehin, who inspired me while I was in boarding school, was the best time. Meeting his lovely wife, Meseret, experiencing her warm welcome, and being surrounded by their children was incredible. Spending a few days engaged in deep and meaningful conversations about life, ministry, and family was an invaluable experience.

They live a life of purpose and run a ministry dedicated to building a healthy family in Ethiopia. Their sacrificial lifestyle and dedication are making a positive impact in the country. Their children, who exhibited good manners, were a testament to the values of hard work, perseverance, and love that Masresha and Meseret instilled in them. This journey reinforced my belief in the power of making a difference and pursuing noble values, and I will forever cherish the memories and lessons learned in Ethiopia.

Since leaving Eritrea, I had been searching for Masresha, the high school teacher who had helped me during my time at the orphanage. I asked many people if they had his contact information, but I still couldn't locate him. In 2017, as I planned a mission trip to Ethiopia, I hoped to find him there. Just two weeks before my departure, I finally managed to get in touch with Masresha through a lady named Adanesh from the USA, who had also been at the orphanage with us and knew us both.

Meeting someone after a long time is like stumbling upon a treasure chest of memories. When I surprised him in Addis Ababa, it felt like an eternity since we had last seen each other. He welcomed me warmly and invited me to spend a few days with his family. I was thrilled to meet his wife, Meseret, and their five adorable children. We dined together, sang, prayed, and expressed gratitude for all the years that had passed.

As we reminisced, I shared that I was still in touch with many people from the orphanage, and he fondly remembered most of them. Our reunion was incredibly encouraging for both of us, filled with laughter, stories, and cherished moments. It was truly one of the best times I've ever had, and I will always treasure his kindness and be forever grateful for what he did for me.

One memorable evening, as I shared my story with his family, one of his children remarked, "You are lucky." When I asked why, he replied, "You have such a wealth of experience." He then added, "What can I say about myself? I have nothing to say." This exchange reminded me of the richness of my journey.

Journey to Poland

Embarking on a journey to Poland in 2019 was a truly enlightening experience, filled with unexpected warmth, hospitality, and moments of profound reflection. The trip, organised by my dear friends Tomek and Wanda, introduced me to the rich culture and history of this captivating country.

One of the most poignant moments of the journey was the visit to Auschwitz, a haunting reminder of the atrocities of the past. The experience was a sombre yet essential one, prompting deep reflections on the perils of dictatorship and the importance of standing up against injustices. It served as a stark reminder of the ongoing struggle for freedom in Eritrea, highlighting the need for compassion, advocacy, and a continued commitment to creating a better world.

Amidst the solemnity of Auschwitz, the vibrant culture and warm hospitality of Poland shone through in unique ways. From sampling the rich and hearty traditional cuisine, such as pierogi and borscht, to exploring the picturesque landscapes and charming villages, every moment was imbued with a sense of wonder and appreciation for this beautiful country.

The connections made with church communities, particularly through Pastor Andrzej and his wife Grazyna, were truly special. Their kindness and camaraderie created a welcoming atmosphere that made me feel at home in a foreign land. The genuine friendships formed during the journey underscored the universal language of compassion and friendship that transcends borders and cultures. The congregation was so passionate for the word of God, and it makes me eager to visit them again.

In the end, the journey to Poland was not just a physical voyage, but a profound exploration of history, culture, and the enduring spirit of humanity. It left me with a renewed sense of gratitude for the opportunities to connect with others, learn from different perspectives, and strive towards a more compassionate and just world.

In 2018, I was blessed with the extraordinary opportunity to travel to Jerusalem alongside my dear friend Rev. Temesgen, a dedicated pastor from the United States. The memories created during our sacred journey to this holy city are ingrained in my being, destined to be cherished for a lifetime. Walking in the revered footsteps of Jesus was a spellbinding experience and visiting the enchanting Garden of Gethsemane left me in silent awe, stirring deep contemplation within me. Exploring the historic Valley of Elah, where the legendary David emerged victorious against Goliath, filled my soul with wonder and reverence.

Having previously encountered these significant locations through the pages of the Bible, the chance to witness them first-hand was truly extraordinary. This pilgrimage not only enriched my understanding but also magnified my reverence for the profound significance woven into these ancient sites. Jerusalem, with its tapestry of rich history and spirituality, provided me with a once-in-a-lifetime opportunity for which I will eternally be grateful.

Journey to the USA

During a special mission journey in the USA, the thrill of reuniting with a childhood friend from the boarding school such as Meseret, Kahsay, Dawit was a moment filled with immense joy and excitement.

Meseret warmly welcomed me to Los Angeles, where our adventure began. Together, we explored iconic landmarks such as Hollywood and the Walk of Fame, soaking in the glamour and history of these famous locations. However, the real magic unfolded as we embarked on a drive from Los Angeles to Fremont.

The landscape of California unfolded before us in all its breath-taking glory. On one side, the vast expanse of the Pacific Ocean shimmered in the sunlight, while on the other, majestic mountains stood tall against the horizon. The beauty of the scenery enveloped us in a sense of wonder and awe, creating a memory that would forever be etched in my mind.

Through Meseret, I had the privilege of meeting her entire family and some old friends, adding another layer of warmth and joy to our time together. The camaraderie, laughter, and moments of connection shared during our journey in California made it a truly unforgettable and wonderful experience. It was a time filled with precious memories and cherished moments that I will always hold dear. Meseret is known for his intelligence and exceptional organisational skills, so California was truly a memorable experience.

During one of my ministry visits to Oakland, California, I was sharing a message about how God works through people, recounting the kindness of Sister Akberet in providing me with food and shelter along my journey. As I shared this heartfelt story with the congregation, a moment of serendipity unfolded when I asked if anyone knew Sister Akberet Tekeste.

To my surprise, a lovely lady named Sister Ghiday raised her hand and exclaimed, "I know her! I can provide you with her contact information." True to her word, Sister Ghiday shared the phone details of Sister Akberet, who, as it turned out, was currently residing in Seattle with her husband.

Filled with gratitude and excitement, I promptly reached out to Sister Akberet and her husband over the phone, expressing my deep appreciation for their kindness and support. The unexpected connection made through the congregation in Oakland opened the possibility of meeting Sister Akberet and her husband in person in the future, God willing.

This serendipitous encounter served as a heart-warming reminder of the interconnectedness of humanity and the ways in which God's grace can manifest through the actions and connections of individuals. It was a moment that underscored the beauty of human kindness and the power of community, leaving me filled with hope and anticipation for the possibility of meeting these wonderful souls face to face.

Tucson, Arizona

Meeting my sister Luchia in Tucson, Arizona, remains etched in my memory as one of the most precious moments of my life. Luchia, with her kind and generous spirit, welcomed me with open arms, and the entire church community gathered to celebrate our reunion.

Luchia's presence radiated joy and respect within the church, and I felt a deep sense of pride knowing that she is my sister. Our time together was filled with beautiful moments and heart-warming experiences.

One of the highlights of our reunion was the daily coffee ceremony, a cherished tradition that holds a special place in my heart. Each gathering around the coffee table was a reminder of the bond we share as siblings and the love that unites us. I will never forget the love and respect they showed me.

Additionally, we organised a family zoom meeting that brought together my brother Yosief and his wonderful family, along with my own wife and children. The virtual reunion transcended physical distance, creating a sense of togetherness and connection that warmed my heart.

The gathering of loved ones, both in person and virtually, underscored the power of family and the importance of cherishing these moments of reunion and connection. Being surrounded by the love and warmth of my sister, extended family, and church community in Tucson made this experience truly unforgettable and deeply meaningful.

Columbus, Ohio

Meeting Nega, my big brother and mentor, was truly a memorable experience. I had the pleasure of meeting his wife, Martha, and their precious children, and immediately felt the warmth of their blessed family. We had such a great time together. I also had the opportunity to attend a service at the church where they serve a wonderful congregation and I was treated with such kindness and respect in their home. Martha's cooking was absolutely delicious, and Nega's humour, cheekiness, and wisdom made the time spent with him unforgettable. We reminisced about old childhood jokes and shared moments filled with both laughter and valuable insights. Spending time with him was a perfect blend of fun and wisdom, and I am eagerly looking forward to meeting again in the future.

Recently, I managed to reunite with Tekue Retta Kassa in Stockholm, Sweden. I spent the whole night chatting, laughing and remembering our childhood. This must be the mercy of God.

My Reflection

"For everything there is a season, and a time for every matter under heaven." Ecclesiastes 3:1

In the intricate tapestry of life, there is a designated time for every purpose under heaven. The moment for refugees and immigrants to be beacons of hope has arrived, their stories not just tales of tragedy but of divine purpose unfolding. Though they may have fled their homelands in fear, they now stand as vessels of inspiration and encouragement for those in despair.

As I look back on the path I have walked, I am humbled by the transformation that has taken place within me. From a place of hopelessness to a position of strength, I now have the privilege of offering hope to others in need. The words of the psalmist ring true in my heart - "be thou my vision, O Lord of my heart." With the eternal light of God guiding my every step, I am filled with a sense of purpose that transcends the material wealth and recognition that the world may offer.

My vision is clear - to spread the message of hope in every corner of the earth. The joy that comes from living a life of meaning and sharing it with others is a gift beyond measure. Despite the hardships that led me to seek refuge in a foreign land, I have found a new home where I can share my faith and story, joining hands with fellow refugees and asylum seekers who have also become ambassadors of hope in Europe.

This divine intervention challenges our preconceived notions of who can be a messenger of God's love. Ordinary individuals, once displaced and marginalised, are now agents of divine grace, bringing light to a world in darkness. Like Joseph in the Bible, we see that what was meant for harm can be turned into something beautiful by the hand of God, saving lives and transforming communities in the process.

The West, too, has a unique opportunity to witness the power of God at work through these unlikely messengers of hope. By embracing their stories and learning from their resilience, we can embody the love and compassion of Christ in our own lives. This journey of faith and service is a beacon of light in a world that often feels engulfed in darkness, inspiring me to continue spreading hope and love wherever my feet may tread.

Immigration has been a longstanding phenomenon, often intertwined with the declaration and advancement of the kingdom of God. This connection is evident throughout history and even in biblical narratives. Take, for instance, a story of Daniel and his three friends who were forcibly uprooted from their native land and relocated to a foreign land, as recounted in the book of Daniel. Their experience illustrates the challenges faced by immigrants, including the confusion of adapting to a new way of life, navigating unfamiliar daily activities, grappling with a language barrier, and being compelled to relinquish their faith, culture, and way of life that had been ingrained in them since childhood. This big change makes them feel like they don't have a place where they belong, just like losing a part of themselves that is as important as a part of their body. However, God transformed their circumstance into a blessing. Finally, Daniel and his friends were a catalyst for the transformation of Nebuchadnezzar, the King of Babylon. I love his declaration, in chapter four, Nebuchadnezzar the king to all the peoples, nations, and *men of every* language that live in all the earth: "May your peace abound! It has seemed good to me to declare the signs and wonders which the Highest God has done for me.

"How great are His signs?

And how mighty are His wonders?

His kingdom is an everlasting kingdom!

And His dominion is from generation to generation.

This is an incredible story."

Who would have thought that such an event would happen to the king of Babylon, at the hands of a young refugee? Well, God works in mysterious ways.

The power of perseverance shines brightly in the account found in Acts chapter 11:19, where we witness the incredible impact of the gospel spreading through a community of believers who endured persecution. Despite the challenges and hardships they faced, their unwavering faith and determination to continue sharing the message of hope and salvation led to the transformation of countless lives.

In the face of adversity, these individuals did not waver but persisted in their mission to spread the good news. Their resilience in the face of persecution became a testament to the strength and unwavering faith in God's plan. It is through their perseverance that many souls were touched, inspired, and ultimately saved.

This story serves as a powerful reminder of the remarkable ways in which God can work through difficult circumstances, using them as opportunities to bring about His divine purpose. Through the perseverance of these faithful believers, the light of the gospel was able to shine forth, illuminating hearts and minds with the truth of God's love and grace. Their steadfast commitment to their faith in the face of adversity serves as a beacon of hope and inspiration for all who encounter their story.

I have a strong belief that this phenomenon will continue to unfold, particularly in the West, with even greater impact. However, it is crucial for both sides to be purposeful and proactive to enhance efficiency and productivity. By taking intentional steps towards collaboration and mutual support, remarkable outcomes can be achieved in advancing God's kingdom.

For refugees and immigrants, in particular, it is essential to adopt a forward-looking mindset rather than dwelling on the past or becoming complacent. Focusing on the future and embracing God's divine plan for their lives can lead to tremendous growth and fulfilment. By being proactive, open-minded, and willing to engage in meaningful work, individuals can unlock their full potential and make a lasting impact on their communities. As William Carey said, "Expect great things from God and attempt great things for God." It is possible. When the heart is ready to listen to God and when the person sent understands the purpose beyond the circumstances, great things can happen.

The power of expectation lies in the belief that when we welcome others with open arms and expect them to contribute positively to our community, they are more likely to do so. It is about creating a culture of inclusivity and belonging that not only enriches our church community but also reflects God's love for diversity and unity among His people. To truly harness the power of expectation, we must go beyond just welcoming people of different backgrounds and actively work towards integrating them into the fabric of our community, empowering them to contribute their experiences and take on responsibilities within the church. This requires courage, understanding, and a commitment to being agents of peace, hope, and good news in the world. By embracing diversity, fostering unity, and making a positive impact in our communities and beyond, we can truly harness the transformative power of expectation.

Personally, my experience at Elim Huddersfield has emphasised the value of genuine inclusion and welcoming attitudes within a church community. The openness and warmth I encountered not only enriched my own spiritual journey but also exemplified God's love for diversity and unity among His people.

While it is heartening to see many churches embracing individuals from different backgrounds, there is a vital need to move beyond surface-level gestures. True integration requires a deliberate and thoughtful approach that not only invites individuals to attend but also nurtures a sense of belonging, encourages them to share their unique perspectives, and empowers them to take on active roles within the church.

Reverse missionary work can be carried out by anyone who has benefitted from the good deeds of others, whether it be from individuals, family members, or organisations. It is simply an act of paying it forward and doing good in return for the good that has been done to you. Many of us have received blessings in the past, and now it may be our time to pass on those blessings to others. Everything happens for a reason, and you are here for a purpose. This is your moment to make a difference and create a better world filled with hope and inspiration.

I want to specifically encourage refugees and immigrants to align themselves with God's vision to be ambassadors of peace and bearers of good news. It is our responsibility to show love to all and to advocate for peace and prosperity in our communities. By breaking down language barriers, promoting unity, and getting involved in our broader community, we can have a positive impact that reaches far beyond the walls of our church. Let us all work together to make the world a better place for everyone.

QUESTIONS AND SELF-REFLECTION FOR PRACTICAL STEPS

The following questions are intended to stimulate your thinking about the chapter's content and assist you in learning some lessons. Please take some time to reflect and absorb useful information. Consider the story's relevance to your own life experiences, let your mind wander, be encouraged to challenge yourself, and look for ways to make the world a better place.

Question 1

What lessons have you learned from this chapter?

Question 2

What are the activities that genuinely make you happy? State them.

Question 3

Can you remember good things that have happened to you? List them.

Question 4

How can you be a 'reverse missionary' and help give back to others?

EPILOGUE

One evening, as the sun was setting and my family gathered in the dining room, we enjoyed a plate of fresh grapes and engaged in various conversations. While my wife and oldest daughter discussed their summer plans, I found myself talking with my two youngest children, Miellaher and Adoniram.

Miellaher, who is incredibly clever and played a significant role in writing my book, truly deserves credit for her unwavering support. During our discussion about the book, I shared one of my life challenges with her, to which she expressed surprise and said, "You didn't tell me this before." I jokingly replied, "That will be for another book." She praised me for overcoming so many challenges, to which I responded, "As they say, what doesn't kill you makes you stronger." It was then that Miellaher reminded me that philosopher Friedrich Nietzsche was the original author of that quote.

The conversation took a humorous turn when my son teased me about my eventful life, asking if that was what I meant when I said life was great. This led to playful banter between my daughter and son, creating a chaotic yet lively atmosphere in the dining room.

Abseri reprimanded her siblings for being boisterous, but she quickly joined in on the fun when they started playing. While Senayit and I were watching and laughing, our cat wandered in through the open door and began meowing for food as soon as he entered the room. Senayit went to feed him. As I watched the scene play out, I couldn't help but think about my own life.

Even though there are many people who are both stronger and smarter than I am, I couldn't help but feel grateful to have arrived at this "promised land" while so many others have not been successful in doing so. Some of them were kept in custody; others passed away in the desert; and others were taken to the coast of the Mediterranean Sea and drowned. My heart was overflowing with gratitude, and Joseph's words perfectly summed up how I felt: "As for you, you meant evil against me, but God meant it for good, to bring it about that many people should be kept alive, as they are today." (Genesis 50:20).

Through my own personal journey, I have gained valuable insights and lessons. I have come to realise that despite life's challenges, we possess the inner strength to forge ahead instead of waiting for others to guide us. When unexpected difficulties arise, they can be disheartening and tempt us to give up, especially if they stem from our own poor choices. However, it is crucial to rise above these setbacks, make necessary adjustments, and redirect our path. It is never too late to bring order to our lives and make amends.

Rather than dwelling on what we lack, it is important to focus on the blessings and resources we already have. I have learned first-hand the significance of reframing our perspective and cultivating gratitude for the present circumstances. Understanding the struggles of personal transformation, I aim to encourage others not to pass judgement on those who are endeavouring to change. Having experienced such journeys myself, I can empathise with the challenges they face and offer support instead.

Each of us has the potential to overcome challenges, embrace growth, and bring about positive changes in our lives. By maintaining a forward-thinking mindset, taking accountability for our actions, and showing kindness to others, we can create a nurturing environment for personal development. It is important to remember that it is never too late to embark on a journey of self-improvement and inspire others with our own experiences.

There was once a young boy who faced immense obstacles upon entering the world. He tragically lost his family and spent his youth in an orphanage. Despite facing persecution from his community, he refused to be defeated. With courage, he embarked on a perilous journey, crossing the Sahara desert and braving the uncertainties of the Mediterranean Sea. Through a combination of divine guidance and his own remarkable qualities, he successfully adapted to a new culture and flourished.

Today, this resilient individual is not only a devoted parent to his three children but also an active contributor to his local community. His unyielding spirit and determination have shaped him into a responsible citizen, fostering a sense of belonging and making positive contributions to his neighbourhood.

This is the story of my personal transformation, a journey that began in Eritrea, was nurtured by the Swiss Nile Mission, and guided by remarkable individuals. The metamorphosis I have undergone, from where I started to where I stand today, is a true blessing that fills my heart with gratitude. I hope that sharing my story will inspire others and encourage them to have faith in God and cultivate a positive mindset.

I am living proof that transformation is not dependent on our circumstances or past experiences. It is a journey that requires perseverance, faith, and a willingness to embrace change. Through my narrative, I hope to inspire others to seek a fulfilling life. With an open mind and the right attitude, there are no limits to what we can accomplish. I pray that my journey serves as a guiding light, motivating others to embark on their own paths of personal growth.

"I will make rivers flow on barren heights, and springs within the valleys. I will turn the desert into pools of water, and the parched ground into springs." (Isaiah 41:18)

Despite a challenging beginning, I have reclaimed all that I had lost and now have a wonderful family. My past has been restored and redeemed. Happiness and gratitude have replaced the negative emotions that once plagued me, such as anger, jealousy, and fear. I am aware of the many blessings in my life and find contentment in them.

My present carries immense significance for me: despite being exiled from my homeland and facing persecution due to my faith, I firmly believe that my life holds purpose and that I am leading a meaningful existence. God has transformed what were initially schemes meant to harm me into opportunities for growth and positivity. This echoes the sentiment expressed by Paul in "All things work for good." Now, having found my dream job, I am able to impact people's lives positively while advocating for those who are voiceless.

As for my future, it is secure. I entrust every facet of my life to God, knowing that my soul is in capable hands whenever I do so. I am confident that the best is yet to come and eagerly anticipate the day when I will come face-to-face with Him. Until that time, I will continue to offer praises to God, who has graciously protected me from harm, redirected the course of my life, and showered me with abundant blessings. Hallelujah! Amen.

SOUVENIR MOMENTS

This picture is taken from our ministry at the Joseph Project working with Open Door to encourage refugees and asylum seekers.

Daniel Habtey was given the opportunity to teach cross-cultural integration through songs and poems in Switzerland.

This photo is taken from the Italian newspaper about the tragedy of Lampedusa.

This photo is taken from Bridge Community Church in Leeds. Working with multicultural and national people is the key for integration. I thank my supporters and the leadership team for their kindness and support to make it happen.

Singing is more than a profession, it brings me joy and there is nothing better than looking forward, hoping for a better future and worshipping God. I thank God for the gift of song.

This photo is one of my favourites as I was introduced to the audience to sing and share my story in Switzerland, to the people who support the orphanage where I was raised. On the television, there is a picture of young orphans in Adi Quala, where I grew up. The director Michael is explaining to the audience that this man used to be one of them but now he came to minister to us. It was amazing to see that their labour was not for nothing.

In Uganda, one of the churches with a big vision reached out to me. I shared my journey to encourage young African people to overcome helplessness.

This photo is priceless. It is my fathers picture which I found from my aunt who passed it to me recently before she passed away. She died during the pandemic together with her husband. It reminds me of his love and sacrifice for his country.

On the right, at the end is my father, just before he passed away. Ghirmay, the man who shared this photo with me, is standing next to him, holding a bag. He told me that my father was on his annual holiday, but when he heard there was a battle, he joined the fight. He ended up losing his life.

This photo is from my best friend Meseret and friends when we started a youth group at the orphanage. This gathering was the result of teamwork and respecting and valuing one another. We were studying, working and singing together. For me, it was the beginning of a great adventure, trusting God and facing and overcoming challenges.

This is a photo taken of the cassette of my second album, during that time there were no CDs. On the right is one of the best musicians, Yosief Y. Ermias who arranged the music.

Vermischtes

Für die Missionsschule in Adi Quala

Der eritreische Liedermacher Daniel Habte war zu Gast in Rossau

Musik und seine spannende Lebensgeschichte – damit hat der eritreische Pastor und Liedermacher Daniel Habte am 21. Februar im «Güetli» ein grosses Publikum in seinen Bann gezogen.

In jungen Jahren verlor Daniel Habte seine Eltern, Grosseltern und einen älteren Bruder und wuchs im Internat der Mission am Nil in Adi Quala, Eritrea, auf. Er denkt noch gerne an diese Zeit zurück. Nach der Schule bildete er sich zum Krankenpfleger aus und arbeitete sieben Jahre in diesem Beruf. Danach fühlte er sich zum Pfarrer berufen. Als er 1997 in den Militärdienst eingezogen wurde, floh er mit seiner Frau und der kleinen Tochter aus dem Land. Der Krieg hatte das

Pastor und Liedermacher: Daniel Habte. (Bild zvg.)

This photo is taken from the local newspaper when I went to Switzerland to ministet and share my story. It was very encouraging for the organisation and the people who supports them.

Adi-Quala: the street that takes you to the orphanage.

The Billy Graham Library in Charlotte, North Carolina.

Meeting my sister for the first time in 23 years in Tucson, Arizona.

Meeting Nega W. Semaet after 30 years, in Denver, Colorado.

Reuniting with my friend Meseret in Los Angeles, California in May 2023

My precious family.

ABOUT THE AUTHOR

Daniel Habtey is a multi-talented individual known for his roles as a singer, songwriter, ordained minister, and commissioned missionary of the Elim Missions and CAM International. He has established himself as the founder and director of the Joseph Leadership Academy, a platform dedicated to nurturing and empowering leaders. His educational achievements include a Masters in Missional Leadership, Doctorate degree in integration studies, along with an honorary doctorate in Christian leadership.

Daniel was honoured as the African Humanity Legacy Icon and World Civility Ambassador in 2022. His influence extends beyond the realm of music and ministry. He has been invited to address government officials and policymakers, delivering impactful speeches at prestigious venues such as the House of Parliament and the European Parliament. His expertise encompasses a wide range of topics, including transformational leadership, social integration, immigration, strategic leadership, and conflict resolution.

Daniel's presence has been felt in various media platforms. He has been featured on prominent mainstream outlets such as BBC Breakfast, BBC Songs of Praise, and BBC Radio 4, where he has shared his perspectives and insights with a broad audience.

Residing in Huddersfield, UK, Daniel finds fulfilment in his roles as a husband to Senayit Alem and a loving father to their three children, Abseri, Miellaher, and Adoniram. His gospel music, often accompanied by his acoustic guitar, has gained recognition, reflecting his journey from his formative years spent at the Swiss Evangelical Nile Mission in Adi-Quala, Eritrea. Throughout his life, Daniel has remained dedicated to his faith, his family, and his commitment to leadership development and societal transformation.

NOTE

NOTE

Made in the USA
Columbia, SC
03 November 2024